Praise for Between "The End" and The Upload

Each lesson was inspiring for any medium, but I want to say thank you for encouraging people to print their books. Holding your published work in your hand is an emotional experience. The information you've shared through the lessons and your responses to our homework have been a great help and I would be glad to recommend your class to anyone who is thinking of self-publishing. The road to self-publishing is a tough road if you do it alone. Thanks for being here for us. ~ KJ Ten Eyck

What a wonderful class. So much information and I have self-pubbed before. I'm fine tuning my metadata and looking at so many new options. Again, an extremely valuable course and I'm glad I joined you. I'd take another class with you anytime. ~ Ane Ryan Walker

Lots of information that I would not have garnered on my own. Your curriculum is well planned. I feel more confident with each lesson. Thank you. ~ J.M. Orise

I've read every lesson & kept them for future reference. This was an amazing workshop chock full of incredibly useful information. Joan is an amazing presenter and teacher. I've taken a couple other workshops by her and I have always learned valuable info & gotten wonderful, important feedback. ~ N. Christine Samuelson

Between "The End" and the Upload

How to Get Your Manuscript
Ready for Self-Publication

Joan Frantschuk
Your Friendly Formatter

Woven Red Productions
Toronto, Canada

Copyright 2018, Joan Frantschuk, updated March 2021
Published by Woven Red Productions
joanfrantschuk@wovenred.ca

ALL RIGHTS RESERVED. Any unauthorized reprint or use of this material is prohibited. No part of this book may be reproduced or transmitted in any form or by any means, electronic or mechanical, including photocopying, recording, or by any information storage and retrieval system without express written permission from the author or publisher. Please do not participate in, or encourage, piracy of these materials in violation of the copyright. Thank you.

All links were tested and true at the time of publication. If you find a broken link, please contact the author at the above address so edits can be made for the next update.

Between "The End" and the Upload is an independent tutorial publication and is not affiliated with, nor has it been authorized, sponsored, or otherwise approved by Microsoft Corporation.

Mastering Word for Fiction Writers IS NOT AUTHORIZED, ENDORSED OR SPONSORED BY ADOBE SYSTEMS INCORPORATED, PUBLISHER OF ACROBAT READER DC, ACROBAT, DIGITAL EDITIONS. "Adobe", "Acrobat Reader DC", "Acrobat", and "Digital Editions" are either registered trademarks or trademarks of Adobe Systems Incorporated in the United States and/or other countries.

Cover and Interior Design by Woven Red Author Services, www.WovenRed.ca
Cover and Header image © John Dakapu via Shutterstock.com

Between "The End" and the Upload/Joan Leacott—1st edition
Ebook ISBN: 978-1-9994791-1-4
ePDF (loose-leaf) ISBN: 978-1-9994791-0-7
Hardcover book ISBN: 978-1-9994791-2-1
Paperback book ISBN: 978-1-9994791-3-8

To all the authors at Woven Red Author Services.

Thank you for asking such good questions.

Table of Contents

Preface 13

Introduction 14
   Retailers Sell to Readers 15
   Aggregators Distribute to Retailers 15
   YOU Publish to Retailers and Aggregators 16

Chapter 1 Polish Your Story 19
   Types of Edits 19
   How Much Will An Edit Cost? 20
      Example Calculation 21
   Finding the Right Editor for You 22
   My Four Favourite Tools for DIY Editing 23
      Word Proofing Options 23
      Websites 26
      Hard Copy 28
      Let Your Computer Do the Talking 30
   When Do You Stop? 34
   Links 35
      Editorial Associations 35
      Microsoft Word Support 36
   Your Assignment 36

Chapter 2 Prepare Your Book 37
   Cover Design 37
      What Genre Is It? 38
      What's It Called? 39
      Who Wrote It? 40
      The Spine and Back Cover 40
      Overall Appeal 41

  About Thumbnails...41
  Print Cover Layouts...41
  How Much Will a Cover Cost?..43
  Cover Sizes 44
 Format Your Book.. 44
  Ebook Formatting...45
  Print Book Interior Design 47
 Revisions 49
 Finding a Service Provider 50
 Links 50
  Informational 50
  Cover Designers 51
  Service Providers..52
 Your Assignment 53

CHAPTER 3 PROTECT YOUR WORK & WALLET............55
 Copyright.. 55
  Intellectual Property 55
  Copyright vs Licence 55
  Who Owns What?...56
  Common Image Licence Types..57
  Register a Copyright...58
  Elements of a Copyright Page..58
  Getting Permission to Use Other Works.............................59
  Digital Rights Management...60
 Identify your Book 61
  International Standard Book Number (ISBN) 61
  Amazon Standard Identification Number (ASIN)...............61
  Bar Codes 62
  Acquiring ISBNs..63
 Piracy, aka Copyright Infringement 64
  Covers that Pirates Hate 64
 Vanity Presses and Scams 65
  Not a Vanity Press 66
 Links 66
  International Standard Book Numbers...............................66
  Stock Photo Licence Samples 67
  Copyright Information...67

  Digital Rights Management Information 68
  Piracy 68
  Watchdogs 68
 Your Assignment 69

CHAPTER 4 PRICE YOUR BOOK 70
 Reality Check 70
  The Tally 70
 The Jargon 71
  List Price 71
  Selling Price 71
  Fixed Cost 72
  Via a Bookstore 73
  Royalty 75
 Ebook Pricing 76
 Print Book Pricing 77
  Direct to a Reader Via Amazon 78
  From the Author at a Book Signing 79
  Expanded Distribution, Yes or No 80
  Summary 81
  Links 82
 Your Assignment 82

CHAPTER 5 PRINT YOUR BOOK 83
 Why Do a Print Book? 83
 The Jargon 84
  Trade or Mass Market 84
  Trim Size 84
  Interior Colour and Paper 84
  Bleed 85
  Binding Type 85
  Laminate Type 86
  Page Count 86
  Pricing 86
  Proof Copy 86
 How Many Copies to Order 87
 Your Assignment 87

Chapter 6 Publish Your Book 88
- Going Wide 88
- Mix and Match 89
- Retailer Account 89
  - ITIN & W8-BEN 90
- Book Files 91
- Metadata 91
  - Keywords 92
  - BISAC Codes 92
- Price 93
- Territories 93
- Links 94
- Your Assignment 94

Chapter 7 Putting It All Together 95
- Step by Step 95
- Tips 97

Appendices 98
- Appendix A: Data Sheets 98
  - Services Used 98
  - Metadata 99
  - Copyright 100
  - Print Book Details 100
  - Pricing 101
- Appendix B: Sample Pricing 102
- Appendix C: The Schedule 104
- Appendix D: Resources 106

About Joan Frantschuk 107

Mastering Word for Fiction Writers 108

List of Figures

Figure 1: Estimating basic copyediting fees 22
Figure 2: Word Read Aloud 31
Figure 3: Access the Speak function 32
Figure 4: Adobe Read Out Loud 33
Figure 5: Fonts by genre 39
Figure 6: Print cover layouts 42
Figure 7: Comparing cover sizes 44
Figure 8: Five giveaways to good design 48
Figure 9: ISBN and bar code 62
Figure 10: Retail cover and ARC cover 65
Figure 11: Cost to prepare a book 70
Figure 12: Comparing print book royalties 81
Figure 13: Publisher compensation calculation 102
Figure 15: KDP print book pricing 103
Figure 14: Print & ship calculation 103
Figure 15: KDP print book pricing 103

Preface

Back in 2004, when I was writing my first novel, the only way to get published was to attract the attention of a literary agent who would, in turn, attract the attention of an editor at a publishing house. Three years later, Amazon launched Kindle Direct Publishing and publishing changed forever.

In 2012, after I'd written my second novel, I ran out of patience with the traditional route to publishing and looked at self-publishing.

A black hole opened at my feet; summed up by the question, "What does a publisher do in order to release a book, and how do I do that for myself?"

After digging deep into the internet, I learned how to publish my books. In 2013, I established Woven Red Author Services to provide formatting services to the growing population of self-published authors.

In conversations with my clients, the same questions repeatedly came up. To share the explanations, I posted articles to my website.

This book is a compilation of those articles with lots of extras. It's part workbook with assignments at the end of each chapter to consolidate your learning and give you some real life take-aways. Also included are five checklists and a 26-step schedule to get from finishing your first draft to clicking the Publish button on a retailer's website.

Joan Frantschuk
Toronto, Canada

Introduction

Congratulations! You've just typed "The End" after a long journey through the creative process. Now you want to get published. You know about the traditional publishers. You've heard about the success and the struggle of self-publishing. You want to know more before you decide on which path to pursue.

Or you're already self-published and you're still confused about the process.

Wherever you're at, you have questions. Where do I go from here? How do I get my book on the shelves, electronic or bricks & mortar? Where should I load my files? What kind of files do I need? What needs to be done before I announce my release date?

In this book, consisting of lessons, assignments, and worksheets, we'll answer the endless questions between typing "The End" and pushing the Publish button on a vendor's website.

Topics include:

- **Polish**: Find the right editor for you. Learn four copyediting methods that you can do on your computer.
- **Prepare**: Cover designers, formatters, narrators, there's lots of ways to spend your money. Why, who, when, how much to pay? Where do you find them?
- **Protect**: Do you need to register a copyright? What are ISBNs? Who owns what piece of your book? Is piracy preventable?
- **Price**: Pick a number, any number? Ebook and print book pricing models are explained.
- **Print**: Trimming, binding, bleeding... the jargon explained.
- **Publish**: How many ways can you sell a book? Go wide or exclusive? To print or not to print?

The sequence of steps is interdependent. You need an ebook cover to format an ebook file. For a print book the sequence is reversed; you need the number of formatted pages before you can create a cover.

The most important thing to understand about publishing is that it's a business; money is involved. You don't go into any business expecting to lose money. Nor do you want to skimp on services that could make or break your career.

Before we begin, there are three important roles you need to understand.

Retailers Sell to Readers

Amazon, Kobo, Apple Books, et al are marketplaces; they are not publishers.

You load your book to their website. They sell your books directly to readers in return for a percentage of the selling price.

Aggregators Distribute to Retailers

Draft2Digital, Smashwords et al are aggregators; they are not publishers.

Aggregators are middlemen. You load your book to their website, and they load your book to retailers. They may charge a flat fee for the load or take a percentage of sales.

Kindle Direct Publishing (KDP) and IngramSpark are printers and distributors; they are not publishers.

KDP is the book printing and distribution subsidiary of Amazon. Ebooks loaded to KDP are distributed exclusively to the Amazon marketplace.

IngramSpark is the printing and distribution arm of Ingram Book Group LLC catering to self-publishers. Ingram Book Group serves all publishing houses around the world, large, small, and indie. They sell ebooks and print books.

OverDrive is an ebook aggregator distributing specifically to libraries; they are not a publisher.

YOU Publish to Retailers and Aggregators

You are the self in self-published, the independent in indie-publishing. Just like the publisher Harper Collins, you control your content, covers, formats, release dates, prices, promotion—the works. You pay the freelancers. You pay the retailers, aggregators and printers. You pay the taxes. You bank the profits.

You are a Publisher! Yes!

Between "The End" and the Upload

Chapter 1
Polish Your Story

In writing, the three most important words after backup, backup, backup are edit, edit, edit. Everyone wants to write an unforgettable story that will hit every bestseller list.

If your reader stumbles over spelling and grammar errors, gets bored by a sagging middle, doesn't believe your characters' motivations and actions... be thankful if all they do is throw your book against the wall and move on to the next book in their TBR pile.

To keep your book in your readers' hands, you must get your book edited. No exceptions.

TYPES OF EDITS

There are a lot of confusing terms that are used interchangeably and, sometimes, incorrectly.

Edits come in two basic flavours: big picture "will this story work?" developmental edits and "is this well-written?" manuscript edits.

Developmental edits analyze the flow of a story. You may have to re-write, delete, and re-arrange whole chunks of a story to keep it moving smoothly and eliminate sagging middles.

Manuscript editing, what most writers call editing, includes line edits, copy edits, and proofreading. These edits are often simultaneous; an editor may correct your grammar and punctuation at the same time she's improving your sentence flow.

A complete edit will often require several passes, so be prepared for the process to take some time.

Understanding the levels will help you negotiate with an editor so that you get what you pay for.

Here are some references to experts in the field.

www.RomanceRefined.com
http://www.romancerefined.com/types-of-editing.html
Even though it says romance in the title, this article covers all works of fiction.

www.TheBookDesigner.com
https://www.thebookdesigner.com/2014/04/4-levels-of-editing-explained-which-service-does-your-book-need/
This is a slightly different viewpoint that makes sense of the confusion of terms.

www.edittorrent.blogspot.ca
http://edittorrent.blogspot.ca
This blog is written by Alicia Rasley, an English professor who is also a published fiction author. Her explanations are great and her book *The Power of Point of View* really made me think about my fiction writing.

www.PeterGinna.com
https://peterginna.com
What Editors Do: The Art, Craft, and Business of Book Editing, edited by Peter Ginna. If you want to go deeper, this is a collection of essays from publishing professionals.

How Much Will An Edit Cost?

Edits are the most expensive part of getting your story ready to publish. They are also the most important part of your success as an author.

Skipping edits is a false economy. You may sell one copy with a beautiful cover and an exciting blurb, but if a reader can't make sense of your story, that will be the only book you ever sell to that reader. She, and her friends, are gone forever.

Chapter 1
Polish Your Story

A freelance editor is not the same as an editor that works for a publishing house. The freelancer will not publish your book, nor will she act as an agent. You pay her, and her job is done. If you see a person acting as both a freelance editor and an agent, tread carefully as there's a potential conflict of interest.

Let's get to those numbers. Editorial fees are based on three things:
1. Type of edit you need
2. Fee associated with that type of edit, either an hourly fee per page or a per word fee
3. Word count and page count of your manuscript

The Editorial Freelancers Association (https://www.the-efa.org/rates/) quotes the going rate for a *basic* copyedit as $30 to $40 per hour at an estimated speed of 5 to 10 pages per hour.

Pages are counted in units of 250 words. The page count on your computer may vary depending on font face, size, page margins etc. Doesn't matter. For editors, one page is 250 words.

Some editors will charge a fraction of a penny per word, typically from $0.016 to $0.038 ($16 to $38 per 1K words).

Example Calculation

Your manuscript is 80,000 words. As shown in Figure 1, a basic edit would cost $1,505 to $2,000.

Yes, it's sticker shock and you may need more than one pass, but you want your story to be the best that it can be for the best career that you can get.

The surprise element might come from the state of your manuscript which in turn dictates the pages per hour that an editor completes. If your manuscript is a real mess, the fee will be significant. A substantive, aka developmental, edit, at the going rate of $40 to $60 per hour and an estimated speed of 1 to 6 pages per hour, would cost $5,333.

In the section "My Four Favourite Tools for DIY Editing", you'll find some ways to possibly reduce this cost.

Calculating an hourly per page fee:

80,000 words divided by 250 words per page is 320 pages
80,000 / 250 = 320 pages

320 pages divided by the average 7.5 pages per hour is 43 hours
320 / 7.5 = 42.67 rounded to 43 hours

43 hours times the average basic edit of $35 per hour is $1505
43 x $35 = $1,505

Calculating a per word fee:

80,000 words times a rate of $.025 per word
80,000 x $.025 = $2,000

Figure 1: Estimating basic copyediting fees

Finding the Right Editor for You

The most reliable way to find an editor is word of mouth. Ask other writers who they use, read the copyright page and acknowledgements in your favourite author's book. Don't forget to ask Google.

Being specific in your search requirements will help you find the perfect match. The most important match in your search is genre. If you write paranormal romance, seek out paranormal romance writers for references. Check an editor's website and social media for preferred genres. Don't expect a non-fiction editor to help you out with your sci-fi novel.

Know what type of edit you're looking for, developmental, copyedits, proofread. Discuss your expectations before you sign the contract.

Many editors will offer a free or low-fee sample edit. This will confirm your expectations. One editor I heard about used a sample of another author's work. You want to see what an editor will do with *your* work, not someone else's.

Prepare to be critiqued and revised. This can hurt and that's okay. When you get your manuscript back, read it over once, set it aside for a few days, then go back to it with open eyes. Don't argue with each and every suggested change. Accept these in the spirit they are meant, to make your story better. Remember, you chose this person and you paid her to do this.

Allow plenty of time for several cycles of edits. Some advice learned the hard way… don't announce a release date until your book is completely done, edited, covered, and formatted. You, and those you hire, don't need the pressure.

And finally, pay fully and promptly. Just because you don't like what she says, doesn't mean she hasn't done her job.

My Four Favourite Tools for DIY Editing

Nothing beats the benefit of a good developmental edit to point out plot holes, sagging middles and blurry character development. I wouldn't publish without one. And neither should you.

But it's so expensive!

You may be able to save some money by creating your own editing process before you submit your work. These are my four favourite tools to help me polish my manuscripts.

Word Proofing Options

Make friends with Microsoft Word, you'll never regret it. There are several apps that mimic Word's options, but why spend money when you can get the functions for free.

Click on File > Options > Proofing then look for the relevant buttons.

The option settings are global, meaning they apply to all of your Word documents from now on, even older docs.

If it doesn't seem to be working, check the settings at the bottom of the Proofing page. Spelling and grammar checking may have been turned off for the document.

Correcting as you go along will save great slabs of time and you'll learn spelling and grammar as you go along. It will also allow your editor to focus on your story and not be bogged down by missing commas and poor grammar.

AutoCorrect

You're familiar with autocorrect on your phone and the inadvertent, and sometimes hilarious, assumptions that apps make. Word does the same. Those funny substitutions don't mean you turn off Word's AutoCorrect; it's far too valuable to ignore.

On Word's AutoCorrect tabs you'll find:
1. seven AutoCorrect options
2. twelve AutoFormat options
3. fourteen AutoFormat As You Type options.

Among those options, you can set up punctuation AutoFormats like:
1. replace straight quotes with curly quotes. Set on both AutoFormat and AutoFormat As You Type tabs.
2. replace two dashes (--) with an em-dash (—). Set on both AutoFormat and AutoFormat As You Type tabs.
3. capitalize first words of sentences.

You can also add your own items to the AutoCorrect list, such as:
1. shortcuts for frequently used words or phrases, e.g., your character or place names
2. words that you frequently misspell but aren't on Word's list.

Correcting Spelling and Grammar

Turn these options on and set them up for fiction writing. Then pay attention to the red and green underlines that identify:
1. spelling errors in the language set for your computer or, optionally, in each document
2. punctuation errors like comma placement or two spaces

after a period
3. subject-verb agreement like "A bubble floats." and "Four bubbles float."
4. and many other items most of which I don't understand but tick anyway.

If you get the red wavy underline under words that are real, e.g., names of people and places, or you invent words for your worlds, you can add these words to the dictionary. Then Word will catch those typos as well.

Writing Style

Think of this as high-level grammar checking. The ones that break my brain to find, never mind figure out. Select the Grammar & Refinements option for a huge and constantly updated array of options. Set them up for fiction writing. Then pay attention to the blue underlines. Those underlines will flag:
1. misused words like there, their, and they're or its and it's
2. run-on sentences
3. incorrect hyphenation
4. when numbers should be spelled out rather than presented as numerals, e.g., twenty-two vs 22.
5. and many other items.

Not Every Error is Caught

Word won't catch every single error you make. If a legitimate word is used in an acceptable way, Word won't throw up a wavy line.

My favourite typo of all time is "carrion luggage". Can you imagine the smell?!

Not Every Error is Correct

Word sometimes reports an error that isn't an error within the context of the sentence. Dialogue or internal monologue in a character's unique voice is a frequent source of grammar errors. We don't always think and speak in perfect English. The most common error-that-isn't-an-error is the flagging of a comma required after "so" and "then" and similar introductory phrases, e.g., "So then I went to the store." Technically commas are required after both words, but in reality, we don't pause when we actually say them.

Websites

My second favourite is a collection of many things, all the fabulous websites out there created to guide and inform writers.

Autocrit.com

It's like having a savvy unbiased critique partner at your command. It's more sophisticated than Word proofing options, e.g., it compares nearby text for repetitions plus you can do a critique by genre. I use it myself and highly recommend it. Yes, it costs money, but it's way cheaper than a copyeditor or proofreader. I honestly cannot say enough about how valuable I find this resource; and it just keeps getting better.
    https://www.autocrit.com/

Style Guides

A style guide is a set of standards to create uniformity in writing style, usage, and grammar across many documents. It is an editor's rule book. At the moment, there are 24 universally accepted style guides listed on Wikipedia. Not all editors use the same guides though they'll have their favourite.
    https://en.wikipedia.org/wiki/List_of_style_guides
    To make your life easier when working with an editor, talk to her about her chosen style guide and try using the same one. My choice is *The Chicago Manual of Style*. CMOS has recently begun blog posts on fiction writing. So even if you don't sign up for membership, sign up for the newsletter for the latest information on correct grammar and style.
    https://www.chicagomanualofstyle.org/home.html

CHAPTER 1
POLISH YOUR STORY

Your Own Style Guide

Whichever style guide you use, the most important thing is consistency.

As the publisher, you can create your own style guide. Well, really, it's your amendments to a given style guide.

The Chicago Manual of Style suggests using what I called a spaced-out ellipsis (. . .) with spaces before, after, and between the dots. The spaced-out ellipsis may break into pieces leaving two dots at the end of one line and the third dot all by itself at the beginning of the next line. Weird, right?

You could use non-breaking spaces, but that's just a huge PITA, so my Woven Red house style uses the Word ellipsis (…) which treats the three dots as a single character that is much easier to deal with and type.

For the same awkward breaking issue, I put spaces after ellipses (…) and em-dashes (—). This keeps the punctuation connected to the prior word, but allows your computer, your PDF app, and your ebook app to break lines into nicely laid-out units.

I also use Canadian spellings for a couple of reasons; I'm Canadian, and I like to subtly remind readers that my books are set in Canada.

Grammar Advice

If Microsoft Word or *The Chicago Manual of Style* doesn't answer my grammar questions, my next stop is Grammarbook.com.
https://www.grammarbook.com/english_rules.asp

My next-up grammar site discusses punctuation and grammar. Edittorrent is written by Alicia Rasley, an English professor who is also a fiction writer. This is a great resource for comparing fiction and non-fiction. Alicia also wrote *The Power of Point of View*, a must-read along with Debra Dixon's *Goal, Motivation and Conflict*.
http://edittorrent.blogspot.com/

My favourite dictionaries are:
Merriam-Webster Dictionary & Thesaurus:
https://www.merriam-webster.com

Oxford Dictionary & Thesaurus:
https://en.oxforddictionaries.com

Hard Copy

Reading in hardcopy gives you a different perspective on your story.

If you don't want to kill trees for little purpose, add a date to the page footer along with the page number. Staple the printer's receipt to the front page to validate the footer date. Now you've got proof of copyright date and a backup copy that doesn't fear technology.

Printing Tips

To maximize paper usage and keep the cost down:

In your Word document:
1. text font is Times New Roman 10
2. no blank lines or page break before your chapter starts, use bold, centred text for a visual cue
3. double-spaced, or one-and-a-half spaced, to provide somewhere for you to write notes
4. no spaces after the paragraphs
5. margins .5" all the way around
6. .25" gutter to allow room for a three-hole punch
7. page numbers centred in the bottom margin
8. paper size is standard letter, 8.5" x 11"

At your local printer:
1. paper is standard letter size, 8.5" x 11"
2. white 20 lb bond paper
3. double-sided printing
4. black & white, no colour
5. three-hole punch

Once it's printed, put your manuscript in a three-ring binder.

How much does it cost? Just under $25 for 200 pages at my local printing store. Your cost may vary. Once you've completed the

Chapter 1
Polish Your Story

review, you'll consider the time and money well spent.

Reading Tips

Add some blank lined three-hole punched paper to the binder. Gather a bunch of sharpened pencils and an eraser; you'll be correcting your corrections. Now, go somewhere different from where you write and where you won't be interrupted. Turn off your phone to increase your focus. Read.

Your natural inclination will be to start at the front and work your way to the end. Don't do that just yet. Start at the end and work backwards, one scene at a time— last scene, second-last scene, third-last scene.

Why? To separate yourself from the flow of the story so you can wonder things like:
- Did I set this event up before it happened?
- Did I motivate this action?
- Is this emotion/action/reaction in character?
- Should I foreshadow this event?
- Have I met this character before?
- Can I turn this object into a symbol or talisman?
- Is this phrase my story theme or title?
- Is this gesture a clue to a character's personality?
- Did this guy's eyes just change colour?

You should be able to answer a lot of these questions very quickly during the first run-through. If you have to stop and think and page forward, then you've found something that needs fixing. And that's a good thing.

But don't start editing just yet. Instead, make notes, lots of notes. Add questions to the above list.

Now read your chapters in random order. Revisit the above list. Make some more notes, add some more questions.

Now read your chapters in proper order. Revisit the above list. Answer all those noted questions.

Now go and update your story on the computer. You'll probably find more questions to ask yourself.

This seems like a long, tedious, unnecessary process. Try it once. It will still be long, but never again will you think it's unnecessary.

Let Your Computer Do the Talking

When you read, aloud or silently, you subconsciously autocorrect misspelled or incorrectly chosen words. Prove it to yourself right now with this brain test from https://www.livescience.com/18392-reading-jumbled-words.html

S1M1L4RLY, YOUR M1ND 15 R34D1NG 7H15 4U70M471C4LLY W17H0U7 3V3N 7H1NK1NG 4B0U7 17.

If you can sort out something this complex without awareness, what happens with something as simple as: The boy re-tried her shoe that was come undone.

There are three sneaky errors in that sentence. Some clues, nothing is misspelled and there are no numbers. Did your eyes catch them? Word didn't catch them either.

Because your not-so-clever computer reads exactly what's written, your sensitive ears will catch the hidden errors. Yes, each number in the sample above was noted and read.

There are two ways to do that in Microsoft Word and one with the free Adobe Acrobat Reader DC.

CHAPTER 1
POLISH YOUR STORY

Read Aloud in Microsoft Word

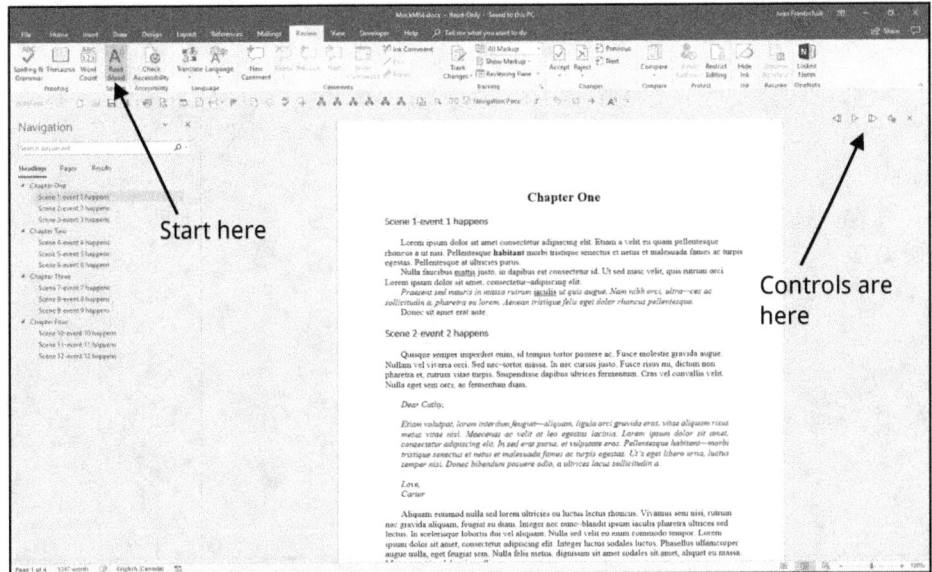

Figure 2: Word Read Aloud

Newer versions of Word have a simpler way of doing things:

Place your insertion point (blinking vertical bar) where you want begin reading.

1. Go to the Review tab.
2. Click Read Aloud.
   a. A control panel pops up in the top right corner of the document window.
   b. In the settings, you can choose the reading speed and the voice.
3. Follow along as your document is being read.
4. Found something to edit?
   a. Hit the pause button.
   b. Do the edits.
   c. Hit play. Be *very careful* not to move your cursor from the play arrow as Read Aloud interprets that as stop reading.
5. Repeat steps three and four until you get to the end and give yourself a pat on the back for making it all the way.

Speak in Microsoft Word

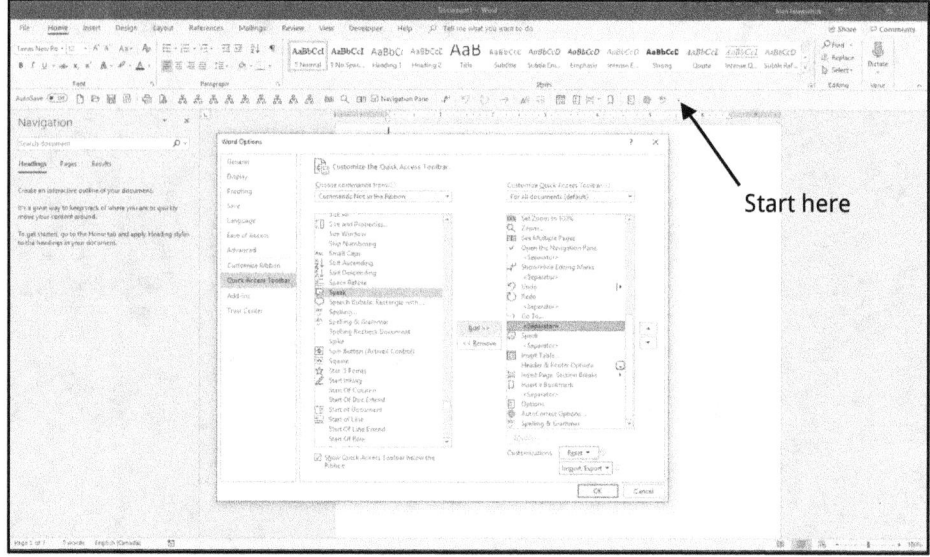

Figure 3: Access the Speak function

In older versions of Word, you have to go a bit further.
1. Click on the tiny arrow at the end of the Quick Access Toolbar. Your toolbar may be above the Ribbon.
2. Select Commands Not Shown on Ribbon from the top-left drop-down list.
3. In the left-hand list, scroll down to find Speak.
4. In the right-hand list, select the command you want Speak to be inserted after.
5. In the middle, click the Add button. Use the up/down arrows beside the right-hand list to move Speak up and down the list.
6. Click OK in the bottom-right corner.

To use Speak:
1. Highlight the text you want to hear.
2. Click on the Speak button.
3. You may edit as the text is being read.
4. Stop Speak by clicking on the Speak button.
5. Repeat steps one and two until you get to the end.

CHAPTER 1
POLISH YOUR STORY

Read Out Loud in Adobe Acrobat Reader DC

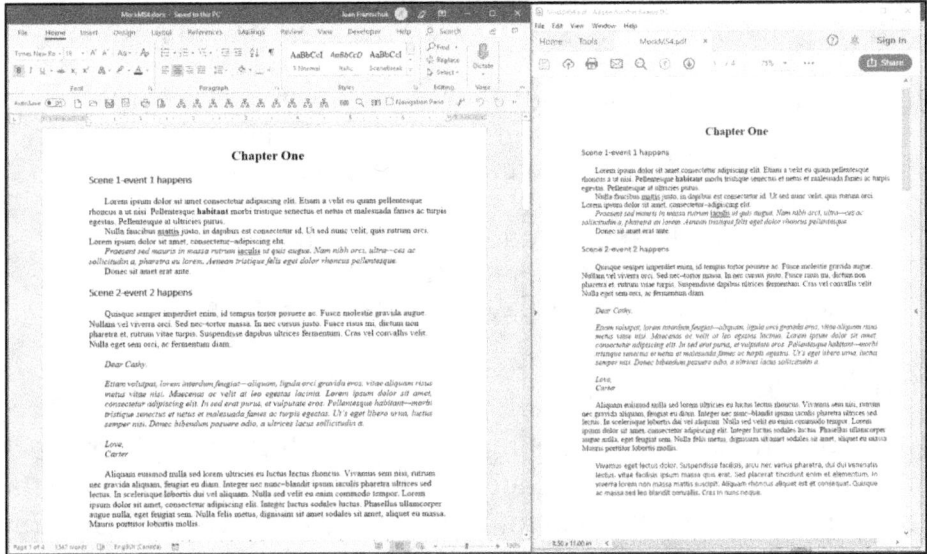

Figure 4: Adobe Read Out Loud

This method uses the Read Out Loud function that comes with the free Adobe Acrobat Reader DC (https://get.adobe.com/reader/).
1. Save your Word document as a pdf
   a. Click File
   b. Click Print
   c. Set printer to Adobe PDF
   d. Click the Print button
   e. Save your PDF file and note the location. This takes a few minutes, so be patient.
2. Set your computer screen to show Word and Reader side-by-side as shown in Figure 4.
3. Adobe Acrobat Reader (Reader) automatically opens
   a. Set view size to Fit to Size
   b. In the View tab, at the bottom, click on Read Out Load
   c. Click on Activate Read Out Loud, reading will start immediately but only read the first paragraph
   d. Ctrl + Shift + B to start reading of the document.
   e. Ctrl + Shift + C to start and stop the read out loud.
   f. Can't hear anything? Check out this thread on the Adobe forum. https://forums.adobe.com/thread/2252795

g. Don't like the voice or pacing? Go to Edit > Preferences > Reading to change things up.
4. As your document is being read from the pdf, follow along in Word.
5. Found something to edit?
   a. Ctrl + Shift + C to stop the read out loud.
   b. Click in the Word window to edit your story.
   c. Do the edits.
6. Click in the Reader window to carry on.
   a. Ctrl + Shift + C to resume the read out loud.
7. Repeat steps five and six until you get to the end.

Listening Tips

To lighten the tedium of this incredibly-worth-it exercise, prepare to be amused at how Read Aloud vocalizes your story, especially the rather flat delivery and attempts at non-English words. Just carry on; this isn't an audio book.

Here are some more tips to make the most of your time:
1. Go somewhere quiet where you won't be interrupted.
2. Use a headset or shut the door so you don't interrupt others.
3. Turn off your phone and any other distractions.
4. Follow along with the read-back to spot homonyms like to, too, and two. Don't jump ahead, stick with the speaker.
5. Listen for when you're confused. Stop and figure out why.
6. Listen for when it feels like the computer needs to draw a breath. Then you *know* your sentence is too long.
7. I save this step for the very last one before publishing. You really want to do this only once.

WHEN DO YOU STOP?

The editing process could go on forever; it's a fabulous procrastination excuse. But at some point, you have to release this book and move on to the next. You're a publisher, right?

Even after all this editing, there will still be typos. You'll find them in many books, traditionally and self published. Your readers will tell you about them.

Don't rush to fix each typo as it's reported and re-release your book. That costs time and money.

Save up the errors and fix them all at the same time. Update your links and reviews. Then reformat your files and re-release annually. Or when your next book is released.

Links

Editorial Associations

Check these editorial associations for a local chapter. Some will connect you to editors via their website.
   Editorial Freelancers Association (USA):
      https://www.the-efa.org/
   Editors Canada:
      http://www.editors.ca
   Institute of Professional Editors Limited (Australia):
      http://iped-editors.org
   Chartered Institute of Editing and Proofreading (UK):
      https://www.ciep.uk/

Join these genre-specific author associations.
   Mystery Writers of America:
      http://mysterywriters.org
   Romance Writers of America:
      https://rwa.org/
   Science Fiction Writers of America:
      http://www.sfwa.org
   Sisters in Crime:
      http://www.sistersincrime.org

These are associations that provide contact information for service providers.

Alliance of Independent Authors:
https://www.allianceindependentauthors.org
Reedsy:
https://reedsy.com

Microsoft Word Support

The grammar and spelling settings in Word are constantly being updated and expanded. To get the most recent settings, see
https://support.microsoft.com/en-us/office/check-grammar-spelling-and-more-in-word-0f43bf32-ccde-40c5-b16a-c6a282c0d251

Your Assignment

Using the notes above, find an editor you think might work for you and note their website.

Based on the word count of your story and the level of edit(s) you think you need, what is the estimated cost for an edit from the person you found?

Find a local print shop for your hard copy DIY edit. Format your manuscript as suggested above. Based on their prices and your current page count, what is the cost for printing.

Record these two expenses in the Services Used chart in Appendix A: Data Sheets.

Chapter 2
Prepare Your Book

Your book is now polished to a lovely gleam. What's next?

Cover design and formatting.

Cover design for your book has two versions, the ebook and the print book. The ebook cover is the front page of the print book cover.

Formatting is a fairly recent addition to a writer's vocabulary. It encompasses file conversion to ebook format and interior design for print-on-demand files.

Some authors add an audio recording. They cost from $1,500 to $3,000 and more, so consider waiting until you've earned enough to meet the cost. A square version of the front cover is required for an audio book. Learn more at https://www.acx.com/ and https://findawayvoices.com/.

Typically, a separate freelancer will do each function, cover and format. Sometimes, you'll find a freelancer who will combine covers and interiors. Book packaging companies will do, or arrange to have done, all three file types, ebook, print, and audio.

COVER DESIGN

"Do I want to read this story?"

That's a reader's #1 question when they view a book on a retailer's website or browse through a bookstore or library.

> A professional is worth every reader who stops to look at your book.

You've asked the question yourself. How long did it take you to reply? As long as a glance takes—a few seconds.

It's that whole judge a book by it's cover thing.

I'm not going to tell you how to create a cover; that's a whole other workshop and super technical. What I want to talk about is how to assess a cover. This will help you choose a cover designer.

In preparation for this discussion, click over to Amazon, and choose two books:
- In a genre that you would normally buy.
- Both are available in print so you can see the back cover.
- One that you would buy on looks alone.
- One that puts you off.
- Try to set aside author name and don't read the blurb.

Now we have some questions to ask of those covers.

What Genre Is It?

Colour and imagery of the background answers this question.

Dark colours will indicate a dark story, bright colours cue a happy ending.

A person running away suggests danger and suspense. A planet in a dark sky has you thinking science fiction. A couple walking hand-in-hand suggests romance. A single object can be fraught with meaning; handcuffs suggest something quite different than a teacup.

Images are often layered to convey multiple genres, a dark street behind a running couple suggests romantic suspense.

Without reading the blurb, consider the following about each of the selected covers:
- Do the covers match the genre in which the book is categorized?
- Does it match the other books in the genre?
- Does it stand out or fade away?
- If it's part of a series, is it obvious? How?
- How many images are used? Too many? Any that don't make sense?

CHAPTER 2
PREPARE YOUR BOOK

What's It Called?

The title and subtitle answer this question. Consider the following:
- Can you easily read the titles?
- Do they stand out from the background?
- If it's part of a series, is it obvious? How?
- Does the font convey the genre?

A book cover delivers a promise about the content, the font supports that promise. If your font goes against the promise, a browsing shopper is confused. Confused shoppers don't buy. Figure 5 shows some mixed-up pairs. Can you tell which font should go with which genre?

Figure 5: Fonts by genre

Fonts used are, top to bottom, Lilac Malaria, Alex Brush, Cervo, Kingthings Spikeless, Edwardian Script, Spin Cycle. Most of the fonts are available at www.fontsquirrel.com.

Who Wrote It?

Consider the following:
- Can you easily read the name?
- Does it stand out from the background?
- Does it stand apart from the title?
- Does the font clash or harmonize with the font used for the title?

The Spine and Back Cover

Often overlooked when judging a cover, the spine and back are also important.

When shelved, most books are spine out. You want the title and your name to be easily read at a smaller size.

The back cover is where the infamous blurb goes along with social media contacts. Typically for non-fiction, the author bio is there as well. The bar code shows the ISBN and suggested retail price.

Often a colour band is used to make the spine text easier to read. These bands can cause issues with printing. Because it's almost impossible to get precise alignment with every single printing of a book, be prepared to accept less than perfection. Or ask your designer to forgo the colour band.

Consider the following:
- If the book were to be placed face upwards in a stack would the spine information also be face up?
- Does the spine information stand out from the background?
- If it's part of a series, is it obvious? How?

Overall Appeal

This is first glance territory—would you buy this book? Why? Why not?
  Consider the following:
- Does the cover clearly state what to expect inside?
- Now read the blurb. Does it match the genre in which the book is listed?
- If there's discord, can you say why?

About Thumbnails

Go back to the retailer. Now play with the zoom until the smallest covers are 1" tall (use a ruler to check). On my big screen, I had to go down to 67%.
  Consider the following:
- Can you read the text in those tiny images?
- Has part of the title gone too small to read, thereby giving a whole new title to the book?
- Have the images and special effects blurred the title?
- Can you interpret the image?
- Can you state the genre with just a glance?

You know it when you see it, the worst cover ever. You also know a great cover when you see it. Now you know why.

Print Cover Layouts

An ebook cover is just the front cover. A print cover will wrap the front, spine, and back of a print book.
  As shown in Figure 6, images can be used in a few ways; a full wrap, or one image for the front cover with a plain spine and back, or two separate images for front and back with a plain spine.

Between "The End" and the Upload

full wrap

two images with plain spine

plain spine and back with front cover

Figure 6: Print cover layouts

A warning about spines that are different from the front and back: resign yourself to getting many books where the spine does not align perfectly with the edges of the spine and one print run *will* vary to the next. It's a tricky thing for a printer to do, so it's up to you to decide how loudly you complain about how small a misalignment. Or think about getting a different cover design.

How Much Will a Cover Cost?

A pair of custom covers by a professional designer will cost anywhere from $150 to $250 for an ebook cover (front only) *and* a print book cover (front, spine, back). You will get a unique cover that will be all yours. If you want to pay extra, you can get exclusivity on the background image.

Pre-made covers are an inexpensive alternative to a custom cover, costing as little as $39. Be aware, that if you love a pre-made cover, so does someone else and you may see your image used by another author.

Then there's DIY, which "the experts" recommend against. To paraphrase Dr. McCoy, "I'm a writer, not a cover designer." Consider the cost of lost sales due to an unprofessional cover vs the cost of having a pro design a cover that works. It's not as simple as you think.

If you really want to DIY, then check out Stuart Bache's cover design course at https://selfpublishingformula.com/design. I've taken it and can definitely recommend it. Be prepared for lots of experimentation and frustration.

Assisted DIY is a bit-of-both alternative. These are websites that provide templates where you can mix and match pre-selected images and fonts. The covers can go for as little as $1. But there's still an amateur doing text placement and font selection; that would be you. Take the training if there's any offered. Study what the bestsellers have done.

Remember that a graphic artist is not the same as a cover designer; it's a whole different art form. If you find an awesome image, consider buying just the image. Most cover designers will work with a provided image.

Regardless of how you get it done, you'll need a jpeg file of the front cover for your ebook and a PDF of the front cover, spine, and back cover for the print book.

Cover Sizes

IngramSpark and KDP both provide free downloadable cover templates. Unfortunately, the two companies do not use the same weight of paper and KDP rounds up to the nearest unit of ten (74 to 80), so the spine sizes, therefore total cover sizes, will differ. Figure 7 compares the template for a 6" x 9" paperback with 400 pages printed on the various papers offered from both printers.

So, if you want to upload to both places, you'll have to pay your cover designer to adjust the overall sizes to create two covers. This likely means an additional fee, so keep that in mind when shopping for a cover designer.

	Paper	Spine	Height	Total Width
IngramSpark	white	.821"	9.257"	13.08"
IngramSpark	creme	.89	9.257"	13.15"
IngramSpark	groundwood	.994	9.257	13.257"
KDP	white	.9"	9.25"	13.15"
KDP	cream	1"	9.25	13.25"

Figure 7: Comparing cover sizes

FORMAT YOUR BOOK

Formatting and *interior design* are used interchangeably. Interior design is used mostly for print books. Formatting is used for either ebook, or ebook and print book together. Formatting also refers to the *layout* of source files (manuscripts) from word processing apps like Microsoft Word, Adobe InDesign, Scrivener, etc.

Ebook Formatting

Ebook files use HTML code to present text and images to a variety of devices; ereaders (Kindle, Kobo, Nook), computers, tablets and phones.

MOBI and KPF Files

KDP has two proprietary files types that add a layer of code to the HTML, MOBI and, the more recent, Kindle Package Format (KPF).

Either file type can be created from Word documents or EPUBs in either the Kindle Previewer or Kindle Create. As an alternative, KDP now *recommends* EPUB files for loading and only *supports* MOBI files.

See more at
https://kdp.amazon.com/en_US/help/topic/G200634390.

A wrinkle in the whole KDP file discussion is that many reviewers still prefer the MOBI file type. So make sure, you get one of these from your formatter or create both as DIY.

EPUB Files

Epub files are used for all other vendors. Use the free Adobe Digital Editions (ADE) to view the files. You can download the most recent version at
https://www.adobe.com/solutions/ebook/digital-editions/download.html.

You cannot view any other file type in ADE, but any ereader device can read these files. Epubs are also used in the public library systems.

There are several DIY ways to convert your book's document file to an ebook file.
- Scrivener has the function built in.
  https://www.literatureandlatte.com/scrivener/download

- Draft2Digital will accept a Word document, then create both an epub and mobi for you to download and use. And you don't have to sell through them to get this service. (https://draft2digital.com)
- I use Jutoh (http://jutoh.com) for epub files.
- Kindle Create will produce a Kindle file from your Word document. https://kdp.amazon.com/en_US/help/topic/G7R2L7V5X6SJH948
- Kindle Previewer will convert your epub to KPF or MOBI. It's a little easier to use than Kindle Create. https://kdp.amazon.com/en_US/help/topic/GUGQ4WDZ92F733GC
- KDP and Kobo will both accept a Word file and will convert it for you.
- There are other apps that will help as well. For a list, run a search for "format ebook" at https://selfpublishingadvice.org/

You can load your Word document for conversion to many of the above apps, but it's not pretty unless you have a correctly formatted Word file. Instructions are available on some sites. Or you can sign up for my own course Mastering Word for Fiction Writers (https://wovenred.teachable.com/) at Teachable.com and learn more than just layout.

Or you can pay a formatter to do it for you. Average cost is $150 for ebook and print book. You will find cheaper freelancers; do check their portfolio and testimonials before you decide.

Beware the Links

KDP and Apple will reject your manuscript if there are links that go to other vendor sites.

You have a few choices to deal with this:
1. Only mention your website and social media.
2. Create separate files for each vendor. This gets confusing and expensive.

Chapter 2
Prepare Your Book

3. Use a universal book link (UBL) to connect readers to your books. Get them as part of the Draft2Digitial service or separately at https://books2read.com/.

Print Book Interior Design

All print books are formatted as PDF files for loading to distributors and aggregators. Some distributors offer the service, but, as I format my own books, I have no idea what the quality is. PDFs created different.

> It's not the app that designs a beautiful book; it's the skill and knowledge of person using the tool.

There are DIY options here as well, the top choices being Adobe InDesign and Microsoft Word. There's no need to spend a lot of money on a subscription for InDesign in the belief it will make a better book. Microsoft Word does beautiful print books.

The average cost for a formatter is $150 for both ebooks and print books.

Either way, you need to assess the results.

Final Page Count

There's no good way to estimate the number of pages your print book will take. It depends on things like trim size, font size, margins, amount of front and back matter. The number won't be known until the formatter is done and you've approved her work.

Good Interior Design is Invisible

Before I started writing, I didn't care who published the book in my hand. Heck, I didn't know the name of a single publishing house.

Self-publishing has altered the author's world.

But readers still don't care who the publisher is, as long as they get a good story.

At a book signing, people are walking right by some of those real books or flipping them open for a quick look and walking away. Why? The story is being judged—first by its cover, and then by its interior design. If the cover or interior is a mess; the story goes unread. If the book is professionally presented, the reader focuses on the story.

Bad design gets in the way of a sale. Good design gets out of the way of your story.

Five Giveaways to Good Interior Design

How can you tell, at a glance, if the print book in your hands has been expertly formatted? Wander over to your bookshelf, or down

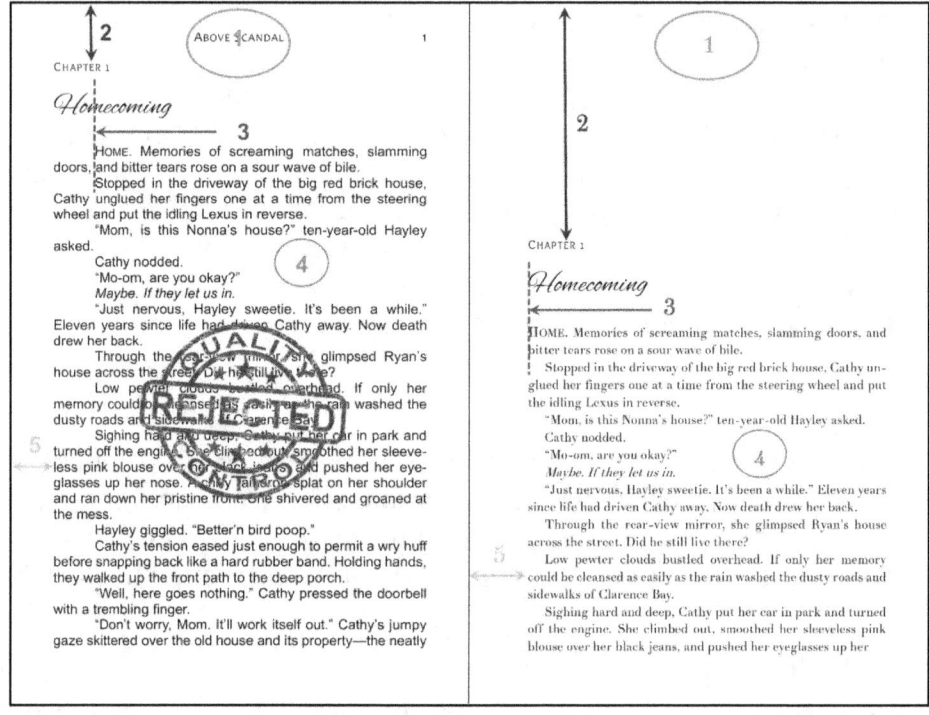

Figure 8: Five giveaways to good design

to the local library, and pick up a book by one of the "real" New York publishers. Refer to Figure 8. Turn to the first page of the first chapter and look at five things:

1) Page Headers

On the first page of each chapter, page headers are correct in their absence. That's right, there aren't any; no author or book title or page number. Just a focus on the text. Page numbers in the footers are fine and can be very helpful for a complex work of non-fiction.

2) White Space
The amount of white space depends on the page size and the font sizes. You want enough content to hook the reader with whatever story you're telling or information you're sharing. All other pages start immediately below the top margin.

3) First Paragraph Indent
Regardless of the presence of drop caps or small caps, the first paragraph has no first line indent. Later in the book, the first paragraph after a scene break often isn't indented either. For all other paragraphs, go for a .2" first line indent.

4) Font Choice
The industry standard is a size 11 serif font though the look varies widely from font to font. More information on serif vs sans serif is at
https://en.wikipedia.org/wiki/Serif.

Some works, e.g., poetry, magazines, reports, use a sans serif font, but a serif font is what readers will expect in a print book.

5) Gutter
To allow for easy reading of a physical book, the inside margins have a gutter added to prevent the text from squeezing into the binding when the book is open.

REVISIONS

Most cover designers will make revisions at no extra cost. That doesn't mean you can get carried away and tweak every little thing. Try to limit yourself to four changes. You want to stay on her good side for the next cover.

Some formatters have standard fonts they use for every project.

If you want to explore your options, find a formatter who will send you examples. Again, don't get carried away and do be reasonable with your requests.

Finding a Service Provider

Just like finding an editor, the most reliable way to find a cover designer or formatter is word of mouth. Ask other writers who they use, read the acknowledgements or copyright page in your favourite author's book. Don't forget to ask Google.

Check out The Book Designer's monthly ebook cover contest.
https://www.thebookdesigner.com/2011/08/monthly-e-book-cover-design-awards/

You'll learn how an experienced professional looks at covers and you may find your artist there as well. Many designers specialize in niche markets. Does he do the genre you're publishing?

When you get to the service provider's website, check out the portfolio. Assess the designs and formats like you've just done for covers.

Links

Informational

Learn more about what you're seeing on a cover.

TheBookDesigner.com: Monthly e-book Cover Design Awards (lots of designer links here):
https://www.thebookdesigner.com/2011/08/monthly-e-book-cover-design-awards/

CreativINDIE.com: Epic List of Best Fonts per Genre:
http://www.creativindie.com/300-fool-proof-fonts-to-use-for-your-book-cover-design-an-epic-list-of-best-fonts-per-genre/

CHAPTER 2
PREPARE YOUR BOOK

TheBookDesigner.com recently released a list of 72 sites for free images:
https://www.thebookdesigner.com/2019/05/72-free-image-sources-for-authors/

Cover Designers

These are a few of the many links to custom and pre-made designs. These links are not intended as endorsements. Do your research, particularly for genre, before you buy.

Canva.com:
https://www.canva.com/create/book-covers/
Damonza.com:
https://damonza.com
GoOnWrite.com:
http://goonwrite.com/index.htm
Robin Ludwig Design Inc.:
https://www.gobookcoverdesign.com/
SelfPubBookCovers.com:
https://selfpubbookcovers.com
TheBookCoverDesigner.com:
https://thebookcoverdesigner.com/shop/
TheKillionGroupInc.com:
http://thekilliongroupinc.com
WickedSmartDesigns.com:
https://www.wickedsmartdesigns.com

Just for fun, have a look at this YouTube video about movie posters. Do you think it applies to book covers?
https://www.youtube.com/watch?v=jwWBQMbMpT4

Service Providers

Associations that provide contact information for service providers.
    Alliance of Independent Authors:
        https://www.allianceindependentauthors.org
    Reedsy:
        https://reedsy.com

People that will guide you.
The Book Shepherd:
    https://thebookshepherd.com
AALEX Author Services
    https://aaxelauthorservices.com/

Check out this link on The Book Designer for an assessment of the DIY Word to ebook formatting services offered by vendors and aggregators.
    https://www.thebookdesigner.com/2019/04/the-convertible-cloud-revisited/

In my own ebooks, and those I format for clients, I don't use fancy fonts or drop caps. There are still so many of the older ereaders out there that just can't handle them. I'd rather a reader tell me how wonderful my story is instead of complaining about formatting failures.

Full disclosure: I'm a Partner Member of the Alliance of Independent Authors, meaning I've been vetted by the Watchdog Desk as offering legitimate, high-quality services. I offer formatting and cover services as well as my course Mastering Word for Fiction Writers (https://wovenred.teachable.com).

CHAPTER 2
PREPARE YOUR BOOK

YOUR ASSIGNMENT

The point to this assignment is to get you thinking like a cover designer, so you can get the cover you want.

Go to https://www.shutterstock.com/home and find an image that might work as a book cover for your current project.

- If you're looking for just an ebook cover, select portrait orientation. If you're looking for an image that will wrap the front, spine, and back of a print book, select landscape orientation. The ebook cover will be the front cover of the print cover.
- If you're looking for a photograph, select photography image type. If you're looking for an illustration, select vector image type. Note: You might have to select the above options repeatedly.
- Use the search function to narrow the search with phrases like "happy older couple", "romantic wedding", "mysterious stranger", "cufflinks", something evocative of the genre, mood, and theme of your book.

For a full wrap cover, look for a focal point to one side of the image, as shown in Figure 6: Print cover layouts.

It can take some time to find a good image; I searched off and on for months for an image for a short story. New images are added every day, so don't give up. Other sites to search are:

iStock by Getty Images:
https://www.istockphoto.com

Adobe Stock:
https://stock.adobe.com

If you're still stuck, your cover designer will help you. If you haven't a clue what sort of image to look for, check out other covers in your genre for ideas.

Be careful of the free photo sites; you can get into copyright and release is-sues.

It's not at all necessary to have an image already selected when you approach a cover designer, but it does speed up the process and helps to communicate what you're looking for.

Copy/paste the URL of the image to Services Used chart in Appendix A: Data Sheets. You'll be sending this URL to your cover designer and it will later be used on the copyright page.

Chapter 3
Protect Your Work & Wallet

Copyright

Before we begin this discussion, I'm obliged to inform you that I am not a lawyer. There are lots of lawyers who blog about copyright issues; these are advice blogs, not a consultation. If you have a copyright problem, please consult an intellectual property lawyer in your jurisdiction. Some writer associations offer legal assistance, so check it out before you pay.

Now for some general information that I've gleaned from my readings.

Intellectual Property

Intellectual property is anything created by the human intellect. Did you know that unique plants created by hybridizing are the intellectual property of the plant breeder? Yeah, who knew?

Copyright vs Licence

A copyright states the ownership of an intellectual property. That ownership confers legal rights regarding that property.

> Copyright = ownership.
>
> Licence = permission = right to use.

You hold the copyright to your story.

A license is the contract that grants the right to others to use the copyrighted property.

You grant a licence to a retailer to sell your book, and to an aggregator to distribute your story. In exchange for this licence, you get paid a royalty.

Who Owns What?

The Story

You own the copyright of your story from the very first word you write, regardless of the tool used, computer, pen, pencil, quill, voice dictation. Your story is yours.

Stock Images for Covers

Stock images used on a cover are the copyright of the photographer or illustrator.

A cover designer buys a license for the right to use the image. The fee generally included the cost of these licenses.

The finished product is a composite image.

Some cover designers retain copyright of the cover and sell you a licence to use it. Other designers, myself included, do "work made for hire" meaning they're working on your behalf to create work you will own. Verify before you buy.

Most stock photography sites request a credit in the form of "cover image by artist's name via website name". In ebooks, this is a live link. This is a request, not a requirement. For my own covers, I include the credit because I know where the images come from. Cover designers typically do not provide credit information for the stock images they use.

Fonts for Covers and Print Interiors

Fonts are owned by the font foundry. Cover designers licence rights to use the fonts on covers. Many licences do *not* include the right to use the font in a logo, so check it out. Watch for fonts that are labelled "free for personal use". This means you can use it for a birthday party invitation or a letter to your nephew. You cannot use it for a book cover; that's commercial use.

Chapter 3
Protect Your Work & Wallet

One client's cover artist had used a Disney font for a pirate-based book. Disney is notorious for defending their intellectual property. So, you can imagine what would have happened if the book had come to their notice. I don't know about you, but I'd rather spend my earnings on a cruise than a lawsuit with Disney.

Working Files

Most designers will not send you their working files because the rights are limited to those who bought the licence for the images and fonts. To get around this, buy the images and fonts yourself and send them to the designer. The designer is then using them on your behalf to create a composite image that also belongs to you.

Songs

Songs are the copyright of the music publisher, not the singer, composer, or lyricist. Most editors and authors will advise against using anything other than the title of a song and its singer, e.g., "Let It Be" by the Beatles.

Common Image Licence Types

In a royalty-free licence, you pay once for the right to use the image for legal commercial purposes (no porn etc.) of which books are one of many uses. You don't pay a royalty each time you use the image. Commercial means used to earn revenue.

You may be able to buy exclusive rights for an image or font, but that will be from the purchase date forward; it does not apply to past purchases by anyone else. Exclusive rights are not ownership. That still belongs to the creator.

> Periodically review the various licences you purchase to ensure they're still valid for your purpose.

Editorial licences are photos of public figures like politicians and celebrities etc., branded items like cars, and, sometimes, geographic locations. These images may only be used for general interest blogs and non-fiction articles. If you want to use an editorial image for a book, you must ask the stock site for a quote on the licence. The one time a client asked, the fee was $2,500 and the person wasn't all that famous.

Stock images displayed on the site are watermarked (multiple logos overlaying the image) to prevent abuse of copy/paste. Do NOT copy/paste an image and remove the watermark; this is piracy.

Be careful about the images and fonts you choose for a logo or trademark. Check if that usage is allowed for each element of each logo you consider. Many of the logo maker sites aren't clear on whether or not they have the right to assign you a licence. Check for disclaimers before you buy.

Register a Copyright

Registering a copyright records a verifiable account of the date and content of the work in question, so that in the event of a legal action, or in the case of infringement or plagiarism, the copyright owner can produce a document from an official government source.

Sadly, a copyright does not prevent piracy. More on piracy later.

Elements of a Copyright Page

The copyright page is on the back of the title page. For a page that is seldom looked at, there is a lot of mandatory information.
- year of copyright, including years of prior publications, e.g., Copyright 2011, 2015 by Amy Author. The copyright symbol © can be used instead of the word "copyright". Using both the word and the symbol is redundant.
- your full legal name or dba (doing business as) name
- disclaimers such as
    - fiction—I made it all up...
    - memoir—my memories may not be what others remember...
    - health—I'm not a doctor...
    - legal—I'm not a lawyer...
- publisher contact information, an email where people can

Chapter 3
Protect Your Work & Wallet

      request permission to quote from your book
- printing history if previously published, e.g.,
Printing History
First Edition: Big Name Publisher Inc.—August 2011
Second Edition: Amy Author—October 2015
- permissions if you used extensive quotes, songs, poems etc.
- permissions if you used graphics from other websites
- ISBNs for each format you issue
  - ebook
  - each trim size of paperback book
  - each trim size of hardback book
  - each trim size of large print book
  - audio book

If you're using vendor-issued numbers, you can skip these.

These aren't mandatory, but it's good karma to acknowledge your team.
- credits and links for
  - photographer of images from stock photography sites. Omitted if you use a cover designer.
  - artist of original images
  - cover designer
  - editor, including prior editors
  - formatter/interior designer

Getting Permission to Use Other Works

For any words or images from sources other than royalty-free sites, you must request permission from the creator or copyright owner.

Often, a polite email will do the job. Sometimes, you won't get permission and you'll have to delete the work and possibly do a re-write.

One client actually got permission to reprint an entire song, "Girl on Fire" sung by Alicia Keys, in her non-fiction book dedicated to helping young girls, so it can be done.

If you're quoting a Bible, the permission will be on the copyright page. Type the permission exactly as stated. If you're quoting from a website, look for their permission requirements.

And then there's fair use, which is a legal way around getting permissions. More info is here https://en.wikipedia.org/wiki/Fair_use. For a general guideline from a writer's perspective, check out "A Writer's Guide to Fair Use and Permissions + Sample Permissions Letter" by Jane Friedman:

https://www.janefriedman.com/sample-permission-letter/

Whether or not permission is required, all works not your own must be cited, or credited, to the creator or rights owner. More info is here:

https://en.wikipdia.org/wiki/Citation.

Digital Rights Management

Digital rights management, aka digital restrictions management, (DRM) isn't copyright. It's computer code inserted in your ebook files to control access to digital material. It's intended as a means to protect a copyright.

You'll see it in action when you want to view an international TV show on the web and you're told you can't access it from where you live. When you buy a book on your ereader and can't view it on your phone, that's DRM.

There are strong opinions on whether or not DRM is a good thing. Some fear it leaves you open to piracy. Some declare it inhibits ebook sales or ebook completion rates. Others say it doesn't matter as it's quite easy to remove DRM.

Study the links provided at the end of this chapter, along with many more you can find on your own, to make an informed decision that works for you.

CHAPTER 3
PROTECT YOUR WORK & WALLET

Identify your Book

International Standard Book Number (ISBN)

The original 9-digit commercial book numbering system was created in 1965 by George Foster, Emeritus Professor of Statistics at Trinity College, Dublin. In 1970, the 10-digit version was developed by the International Organization for Standardization (ISO). Starting in 2005, ISBNs were modified to 13 digits for compatibility with the "Bookland" European Article Number (EAN-13).

The 13-digit version is the 10-digit version plus a 3-digit country code. The complete history of ISBNs is available on Wikipedia at
https://en.wikipedia.org/wiki/International_Standard_Book_Number.

ISBNs are issued by agencies in the publisher's country for each variation of a book; ebook, print book, audio. Epub files and mobi files should each have separate ISBNs, though many authors will use the same ISBN for all ebooks.

All ISBNs are listed on the copyright page for each variation of format. The print book number also goes in the bar code on the back cover.

If you purchase your ISBNs from Bowker, note the imprint name provided in the bottom right corner on the My Company tab. You'll need it when you load your book to KDP.

Amazon Standard Identification Number (ASIN)

An ASIN is a 10-digit *product code* issued by Amazon. In the case of books, the ASIN is the last 10 digits of the ISBN with *KDP set as the publisher*. The registration group identifier for USA and English is added behind the scenes.

Bar Codes

Bar codes are a graphical representation of the ISBN that can be automatically scanned by booksellers for inventory and sales control. Bar codes are displayed on the back cover of print books. They're not printed in ebooks at all as scanners aren't required for ebook sales. Companies have size requirements for bar codes, so check with your issuing agency and distributor/printer.

Bracketed groups are, left to right:
- registration group identifier
- country, language
- publisher
- title
- check digit
- currency
  0&1-Pounds Sterling
  3-Australia
  4-New Zealand
  5-US
  6-Canada
- retail price in designated currency

US$/Canadian$ for use in Canadian bookstores. The same can be done with other currencies.

Figure 9: ISBN and bar code

The list price for your print book can be added to the bar code for the convenience of booksellers. Some bar codes include a suggested retail price with an optional currency conversion which is helpful for booksellers in countries other than the US.

Some authors won't put a price on a print book, thinking that they might change it later. Print prices aren't as fluid as ebook prices. The cost of printing a physical book is fixed, leaving little wiggle room for pricing. There's more about this later in the chapter on Print Book Pricing.

CHAPTER 3
PROTECT YOUR WORK & WALLET

Bar codes come embedded in the IngramSpark cover template and KDP will add the bar code for you, so there's no need to purchase a bar code. But, if do want to purchase one you can get them free, or for a small donation, at www.bookow.com,
https://www.bookow.com/resources.php#isbn-barcode-generator.

Acquiring ISBNs

ISBNs are sold by designated governmental agencies in the publisher's country of residence. Some agencies charge quite a lot of money. Those agencies often offer bulk-buying at reduced rates.

Other agencies offer free ISBNs, e.g., Canada, France. Some authors think to get around the residency requirement for these free ISBNs by having a friend acquire the numbers on their behalf. The friend is now the publisher, getting the credit and legal responsibility for your book. The legal implications of another country aren't something I'd want to take on, so do rethink this idea.

A new thing is individuals/companies taking advantage of hugely discounted bulk purchases of ISBNs and then selling them on to authors at a profit. I'm not sure how this works from a legal perspective, so tread carefully.

ISBNs belong to the publisher who purchases them and then assigns them to the books they publish. This is critical in understanding the reason behind the advice to not use the free ISBN issued by retailers or distributors. The free numbers cannot be used on any other retailer's site, so separate covers are required.

ISBNs track sales by publisher and title. As seen in Figure 5, there is no code in the ISBN for author, only publisher.

When KDP issues a free ISBN, in effect, they become the publisher. So, if a book with an KDP ISBN hits a bestseller list, Amazon/KDP gets the kudos, not you. Fortunately, your author name does show on the list. IngramSpark now offers ISBNs as well.

Does it matter who gets credit? It's your choice, your success, your wallet.

Piracy, aka Copyright Infringement

It's an unfortunate fact of self and traditional publishing; making your book available anywhere on the internet makes it vulnerable to piracy. And it *will* happen.

Fortunately, governments around the globe are starting to fight back.

Can you fight back on a personal level?

Yes.

You can set up a Google alert, https://support.google.com/websearch/answer/4815696?hl=en, for whenever your author name or the titles of your books pop up then go to the offending site and try to find a link that connects to a Digital Millennium Copyright Act (DMCA, https://en.wikipedia.org/wiki/Digital_Millennium_Copyright_Act) take-down notice. Complete and submit the notice and hope somebody pays attention. You could get completely ignored.

But *be careful here* as some piracy sites are a cover for phishing operations and your book is being used as bait. NEVER enter your credit card information.

Another way is to establish an account at a monitoring service that will scour the internet and issue takedown notices on your behalf. If you go this route, check every notification they send you, so they don't embarrass you by issuing a notice to a friend who wrote a glowing review on her blog. Yes, it happened to me. Ugh!

Covers that Pirates Hate

Pirates discover your book as soon as they hit an advance review copy (ARC) site like NetGalley or hit the new releases list at retailer sites. There's not much you can do about the new releases list. Piracy at the ARC sites can be short-circuited by loading a very plain cover for your book. Above are Lila DiPasqua's covers, used with her kind permission. Her cover designer created the ARC cover as well as a classy title page graphic with black text on a white page.

CHAPTER 3
PROTECT YOUR WORK & WALLET

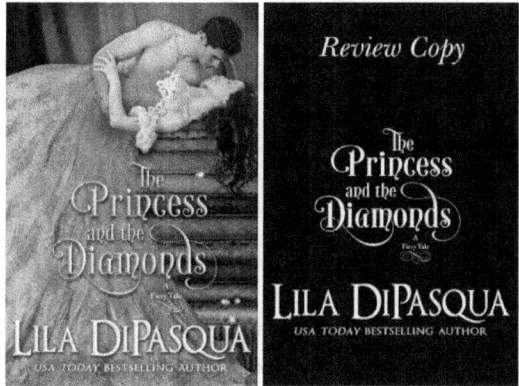

Figure 10: Retail cover and ARC cover

Vanity Presses and Scams

A vanity press engages in predatory practices where they charge a LOT of money (I'm aware of one unfortunate author who spent $11,000) for very little service (the cover and formatting were horrendous). Their customer base is writers, not readers. They sell high-dollar, low-quality services to unsuspecting writers, not books to avid readers. If you see guaranteed sales numbers or promises of hitting the bestseller lists, run far, run fast. That's a vanity press.

> The best protection you have is a healthy scepticism.
> If a deal or offer looks to good to be true... it's probably a scam. RUN!

The hallmark difference between a vanity press and a legitimate publishing house is how the money flows. With a legitimate house, the money flows *towards* you. You don't pay for anything. You get advances and royalties. You keep the copyright. With a vanity press, your money flows *away* from you at a rapid pace, frequently taking all your rights, sometimes including copyright, with it. Fees will start in the low thousands and go up and up and up.

The latest, and most expensive, scam is book-to-screen. The "publisher" will offer various levels of packages; the ultimate being to write a screen play based on your book and present it to

Hollywood insiders. Of course, the complete package will cost a LOT of money.

For real-life information, check out this blog post
https://www.janefriedman.com/how-a-book-becomes-a-movie.

And now scammers are appropriating agents' names and almost-but-not-quite-right agencies.

Not a Vanity Press

Don't confuse the above predators with companies who will legitimately prepare your self-published book for publication and load them to retailers for you. They'll connect you with editors, formatters, cover artists, and marketers. I think of them as aggregators who offer editing and formatting services. They will charge a fee but much less than vanity presses and you keep your copyright. Read the contract carefully.

Also, don't confuse vanity presses with self-publishing. Yes, you pay for freelance services like covers, editing, and formatting, but this is work made for hire. You pay a much smaller fee, you get files in return, and that's the end of the contract. Some freelancers will upload to retailer sites on your behalf; they'll collect a fee for time spent but that's all. Freelancers don't ask for any of your rights.

Vanity presses will often contact you directly, praise your book, and then "beg" you join them. When in doubt, investigate.

LINKS

International Standard Book Numbers

Here's a partial list of agencies that sell ISBNs.
Bowker USA:
https://www.myidentifiers.com/get-your-isbn-now

Canada:
   http://www.bac-lac.gc.ca/eng/services/isbn-canada/Pages/isbn-canada.aspx
Nielsen United Kingdom and Ireland:
   https://www.nielsenisbnstore.com /Home/Isbn
New Zealand:
   http://www.natlib.govt.nz/publishers-and-authors/isbns-issns-and-ismns
THORPE-Bowker Australia:
   https://www.myidentifiers.com.au/Get-your-isbn-now

Other agencies and information associated with any ISBN can be found at the ISBN International website, https://www.isbn-international.org/agencies. Get a handy download at https://www.isbn-international.org/sites/default/files/Register%20of%20ISBNs%20and%20accompanying%20metadata.pdf

Stock Photo Licence Samples

iStock by Getty Images Licence Agreement:
   https://www.istockphoto.com/ca/legal/license-agreement
123rf.com Licence Agreement:
   https://www.123rf.com/license.php

Copyright Information

Wikipedia copyright:
   https://en.wikipedia.org/wiki/Copyright_registration
World Intellectual Property Organization:
   http://www.wipo.int/copyright/en/
Canada copyright registration:
   http://www.ic.gc.ca/eic/site/cipointernet-internetopic.nsf/eng/h_wr00003.html
USA copyright registration:
   https://www.copyright.gov/

UK copyright registration:
https://www.copyrightservice.co.uk/

Digital Rights Management Information

Wikipedia DRM:
https://en.wikipedia.org/wiki/Digital_rights_management
ThePassiveVoice.com on DRM:
http://www.thepassivevoice.com/?s=DRM

Piracy

Digital Millennium Copyright Act Services Ltd. Piracy monitoring service
http://www.dmca.com/
The Passive Voice, piracy articles
http://www.thepassivevoice.com/category/piracy/
UpCounsel online service: DMCA notice
https://www.upcounsel.com/dmca-notice

Watchdogs

Alliance of Independent Authors Watchdog Desk
https://selfpublishingadvice.org/best-self-publishing-services/
Writer Beware, created by Victoria Strauss. Definitely sign up for her newsletter or follow her on social media.
https://accrispin.blogspot.com/
For some case studies and dire warnings, see
https://www.sfwa.org/other-resources/for-authors/writer-beware/cases/
David Gaughran, author and activist
http://davidgaughran.com/blog/

CHAPTER 3
PROTECT YOUR WORK & WALLET

YOUR ASSIGNMENT

Find the organization that registers copyright in your country. Copy/paste the URL to the Copyright chart in Appendix A: Data Sheets.

Note: The US Copyright Office has recently made changes regarding timelines and bulk registrations. Consider acquiring the ISBNs long before your release date using placeholder information until you know the final information.

Chapter 4
Price Your Book

Pick a number, any number? If only it were that easy.

REALITY CHECK

Before we go any further, I'll state the obvious; self-publishing is a business. It sounds mercenary to say your art is for sale. But it is, just like a Rembrandt. May you have many, many readers who will happily pay for your art.

The point of a business is to make money and it comes down to a simple formula: REVENUE − EXPENSES = PROFIT.

The Tally

So, what expenses have we incurred so far?

One round of editing	$1,505
Cover design	250
Formatting	150
ISBN (US)	125
Copyright (US)	35
Total	$2,065

Figure 11: Cost to prepare a book

That's just one book. And *doesn't include* stuff like marketing fees, internet fees, app fees, income taxes, etc. If you're comparing traditional publishing to self-publishing, these extra expenses are common to both, so you would still need to pay them with whatever advances and royalties you receive.

A successful business pays for its expenses and has money left over for cost of living or fun stuff like river cruising.

To cover these expenses, you have to make sales. The more books you sell, the better you cover your expenses and the more profit you earn.

Note: The total of $2,065 is used in all the examples below.

The Jargon

Like all industries that manufacture a product, there are basic terms, many of which may be familiar to you. Instead of manufacturing a shirt, you are publishing a book.

List Price

Also called suggested list price and manufacturer's suggested retail price (MSRP), this is the price you assign when you upload your book to a retailer. The big publishers will often price ebooks and print books the same. Self-publishers generally set a list price for the ebook at considerably less than the print book, e.g., $4.99 and $17.99 respectively. The list price goes in the bar code on the back of your print book.

Selling Price

Also called sales price or promotional price. If you put your ebook on sale or sell the print book for less than the list price; this is the sale price. After a sale is over, your book returns to its list price.

If an ebook is perma-free, neither you nor the retailer make any earnings. Perma-free is often used to entice a reader to delve into the next book set at a typical list price. It's most effective when there are five or more books to hook the reader.

Amazon frequently adjusts the list price to undercut or price match other retailers. You permit this when you agreed to their Terms of Service. It's usually a small amount, $4.99 vs $4.76. Other retailers don't do this.

Fixed Cost

This is the amount the retailer charges the author to list her book on their site. It's collected only when there's a sale. This is what retailers really mean when they state, "load free to our site". Understanding the impact of fixed costs on royalty is critical to financial success.

Ebooks

For ebooks, the fixed cost is a *percentage* deducted off the selling price.

You won't see the percentage stated anywhere as in, "We deduct 30% off the selling price". Retailers will talk about "your royalty rate is 70%". The two numbers will always add up to 100%.

Amazon Delivery Fee

Amazon also deducts a variable delivery fee to download your book to your reader's device. This is only charged for books that earn a 70% royalty.

There's a long list of fees depending on country. The American/Canadian rate is $0.15 per megabyte. It's deducted before your royalty is calculated.

If your book has a lot of illustrations, pay attention to this delivery fee and adjust your list price accordingly.

Print Books

For print books, the fixed cost is a *dollar amount*. The pricing is more complicated as you are manufacturing a "real" thing. I deliberately say "manufacturing". There are machines involved that need maintenance which are operated by people that need salaries.

Chapter 4
Price Your Book

Plus, the books are shipped out to readers, authors, bookstores, and libraries. These manufacturing costs are often called "printing fees". We'll talk about the various selling scenarios in Print Book Pricing.

Via a Bookstore

This gets complicated because one more person gets a piece of the pie, the bookstore owner. For this scenario, we a couple more definitions.

Discounted Price

Bookstores need to make a profit to keep the lights on, pay salaries and benefits, and stock the shelves. They expect to buy books at a discount, meaning a percentage of the list price. If the discount is 55%, the bookstore cost is 45% of list price.

The big publishers offer a 43% to 47% discount. The bookstore can sell at any price they choose, but if they sell at list price, their revenue is 57% to 53% of list price. As the publisher, you can select any discount.

Your royalty is the discounted price less the printing cost. The author pays for printing, the bookstore pays for shipping, handling, and tax.

Refer to the Publisher Compensation Calculation in Figure 13 in Appendix B: Sample Pricing.

For this example, I've set a list price of $17.99 with a 30% discount. More on the rate later. From the sample calculation, we know the royalty dollar amount (publisher compensation) is $7.67, so we can go straight to the percentage.

ROYALTY % = (ROYALTY / LIST PRICE) x 100
ROYALTY % = ($7.67 / $17.99) x 100
ROYALTY % = 46% of list price

How many books do you have to sell to recoup your basic expenses and declare a profit?
EXPENSES / ROYALTY = NUMBER OF BOOKS
$2,065 / $7.67 = 269 books

What about the bookstore's revenue and profit?
BOOKSTORE REVENUE = LIST PRICE - {DISCOUNTED PRICE + [(HANDLING + SHIPPING + TAX) / 10]}
BOOKSTORE REVENUE = $17.99 - {$12.60 + [($1.99 + $9.30 + $4.86) / 10]}
BOOKSTORE REVENUE = $17.99 - $13.72
BOOKSTORE PROFIT = $4.28 less rent, utilities, salaries, storage, etc.

If your book is sold to a public library, your royalty is the same. But there's no revenue for the library.

Returnable vs Non-returnable

Another bookstore expectation is that your book is returnable. This means if the store doesn't sell any of the copies they ordered, the books can be returned to the distributor for a refund issued by the publisher, who, in turn, reduces the author's payment.

Returned books can either be sent to the author at the author's expense. Or the bookstore can strip the covers for credit and destroy the books locally.

This creates a potential loss.

I have heard of authors taking a huge hit when stores order a whole pallet of books, never unpack them or shelve them, and then return the entire order untouched. It's a huge risk.

A well-respected, best-selling author who devotes a lot of time to author education suggests a discount of 30% with no returns. This is based on the most-likely scenario that your book will be ordered for a specific customer or a special event rather than on the bookstore owner's speculation that your book will be sold. It's a potential hazard neatly avoided.

Chapter 4
Price Your Book

Selling at Barnes & Noble

Books loaded to IngramSpark can be considered for in-store placement at Barnes & Noble. See their criteria here:
https://help.ingramspark.com/hc/en-us/articles/360007196872-Barnes-Noble-Requirements.

Selling at Chapters Canada

Canada's largest bookstore chain is open to self-publishers. See their criteria here:
https://www.chapters.indigo.ca/en-ca/authors-faq/?link-usage=Footer%3A%20Vendors%20%26%20Authors
A Canadian dollar price is needed on the barcode.

Royalty

Royalty is the publishing-industry word for payment to the author for each book sold. It's generally stated as a percentage of whatever the price, list or sales, the book sold at.

> The math guides the marketing.

Amazon is an online retailer. Kindle Direct Publishing (KDP) is Amazon's self-publishing business. The terms KDP and Amazon are used interchangeably in the self-pub industry.

Ebooks

Royalty is stated as a percentage, 70% being the standard for most ebook vendors.
KDP has either a 35% or 70% royalty rate based on certain conditions of book price and marketplace (where the book is sold).
https://kdp.amazon.com/en_US/help/topic/G200634560
KDP offers KDP Select, where you can schedule free download days, and Kindle Unlimited which is a lending program. Pros and cons are much debated for these programs. The main pro is supposedly more exposure. The main con is that KDP demands exclusivity on their site.

https://kdp.amazon.com/en_US/select

Finally, you can sell books on your own website using an ecommerce platform like Shopify. Royalties can go as high as 95% but you may have to deal with global sales tax collection and payment. Check with the platform provider.

Print Books

Royalty for print books is stated as a *dollar amount* for self-publishers. To find out the percentage, get out your calculator and follow the examples below.

Ebook Pricing

Because an ebook is an electronic asset, things are relatively straightforward. Amazon charges a delivery fee and, even though it's *only* a few pennies, the delivery fee comes off your royalty.
ROYALTY = LIST PRICE x FIXED PERCENTAGE
ROYALTY = $4.99 x 70%
ROYALTY = $3.49

A book of 100K words is roughly 1.3 KB after conversion to the KDP format. To include the Amazon delivery fee, you get:
ROYALTY = (LIST PRICE – DELIVERY FEE) x FIXED PERCENTAGE
ROYALTY = ($4.99 – (1.3 KB x $0.15)) x 70%
ROYALTY = ($4.99 – $0.20) x 70%
ROYALTY = $3.35

Sure, a $0.20 drop doesn't seem like much, but it does add up; 1,000 books sold reduces your total royalty by $140.
(1000 x ($3.49 - $3.35))

CHAPTER 4
PRICE YOUR BOOK

Or if you put your book on sale for $0.99 in hopes of selling enough copies to recoup earnings and hitting a best-sellers list:
ROYALTY = SALE PRICE x FIXED PERCENTAGE
ROYALTY = $0.99 x 35%
ROYALTY = $0.35

How many books do you have to sell to recoup your expenses before you can declare a profit?
EXPENSES / ROYALTY = NUMBER OF BOOKS
At the regular price: $2,065 / $3.49 = 592 books
After the delivery fee: 2,065 / 3.35 = 617 books
At the sale price: $2,065 / $0.35 = 5,900 books

Bit of a shocker, isn't it? And that doesn't include those other expenses. Now you know why a marketing plan is so important.

PRINT BOOK PRICING

The publisher (that's you, remember) wants to balance a lower price to get the most sales with a higher price to maximize profit. It boils down to what a reader is willing to pay.

Would you pay $17.99 for a print book by your favourite author?

Probably not for a mass-market book, sized at approximately 4" x 6". But there is more price tolerance for a physically larger book which is why self-publishers sell trade paperbacks sized between 5" x 8" to 6" x 9".

As you play with the pricing tools shown below, you'll see, or work out, a minimum list price, the smallest price you can assign to your book to earn the smallest profit. You might be tempted to set this price in hopes of better sales. Don't do this to yourself; your story-telling skills are worth more than that.

If you want a fair price, research the best-sellers in your genre near your page count. If you're a debut author, consider setting your price at $2 less. As you become better-known, you can increase your prices. If you're a best-seller, match the price point.

There are three common scenarios in which a book gets from the author to the reader. As we examine each scenario, we'll see that different list and sales prices work best for different scenarios.

As stated earlier, the formula uses dollars, rather than percentages, and shipping is sometimes included in the fixed cost.

ROYALTY = LIST PRICE − FIXED COST

Direct to a Reader Via Amazon

IngramSpark does not sell direct to the public.

KDP uses a percentage similar to the ebook formula.
ROYALTY = (ROYALTY RATE x LIST PRICE) − PRINTING COSTS

Refer to KDP Royalty Calculator in Figure 15 in
Appendix B: Sample Pricing. For more information, check out the KDP help documents at
https://kdp.amazon.com/en_US/help/topic/G201834330

The KDP royalty rate is 60% of list price, reduced by the printing costs, when books are sold direct to a reader. The author pays to print the book (fixed cost). The reader pays for shipping and taxes.
ROYALTY = (ROYALTY RATE x LIST PRICE) − PRINTING COSTS
ROYALTY = (60% x $17.99) − $4.45
ROYALTY = $10.80 − 4.45
ROYALTY = $6.35

And here's the royalty rate after expenses.
ROYALTY % = (ROYALTY / LIST PRICE) x 100
ROYALTY % = ($6.35 / $17.99) x 100
ROYALTY = 35%

Chapter 4
Price Your Book

How many books do you have to sell to recoup your basic expenses and declare a profit?

EXPENSES / ROYALTY = NUMBER OF BOOKS

$2,065 / $6.35 = 326 books

From the Author at a Book Signing

The author pays to have the books printed and shipped to her home so she can sell them to readers at book shows and signings.

Cutting out the middleman allows you to offer the book at a special a rate and still make a profit. Just make sure you cover the cost of the import duties, currency exchange rates, table rental, gas, food and drink, payment processing fees, etc.

Refer to the Print & Ship Calculation in Figure 14 in

Appendix B: Sample Pricing. The numbers are from IngramSpark because they include taxes and shipping. An order of ten books is used for a real-life feel.

For this example, I've set a special conference sale price of $10.00. I've *haven't* altered the bar code. I *have* made up a sign to advertise the reduced amount, saving the reader $7.99 off the list price. What a bargain! And giving change is so much easier.

First, we calculate the royalty in dollars. Duties, currency exchange, and sales tax are set to zero for simplicity.

ROYALTY = SALE PRICE − (PRINTING COST + SHIPPING + TAXES + DUTIES + CURRENCY EXCHANGE + SALES TAX)

ROYALTY = $10.00 − ($65.35 / 10)

ROYALTY = $3.47

Then as a percentage.

ROYALTY % = (ROYALTY / SALES PRICE) x 100

ROYALTY % = ($3.47 / $10.00) x 100

ROYALTY = 35% of sales price

How many books do you have to sell to recoup your basic expenses and declare a profit?
EXPENSES / ROYALTY = NUMBER OF BOOKS
$2,065 / $3.47 = 595 books

Expanded Distribution, Yes or No

On KDP, you'll see the option "Expanded Distribution". KDP works with large *US only* distributors to make your book available for libraries and bookstores to order. Of course, they take a sizable cut. The purchaser pays for shipping and taxes.

The KDP Expanded Distribution royalty rate is 40%, reduced by the printing costs, for expanded distribution.
ROYALTY = (ROYALTY RATE x LIST PRICE) – PRINTING COSTS
ROYALTY = (40% x $17.99) – $4.45
ROYALTY = $7.20-$4.45
ROYALTY = $2.75

Recalculated to show the true royalty percentage.
ROYALTY % = (ROYALTY / SALES PRICE) x 100
ROYALTY % = ($2.75 / $17.99) x 100
ROYALTY = 15%

How many books do you have to sell to recoup your basic expenses and declare a profit?
EXPENSES / ROYALTY = NUMBER OF BOOKS
$2,065 / $2.75 = 751 books

Given the threat of Amazon to their own businesses, many bookstores and libraries are reluctant to order books from KDP.

This is why many authors will forgo KDP Expanded Distribution (don't tick the box) and use IngramSpark for paperback and hardback distribution. Likely, the bookstore already has accounts at Ingram as well.

CHAPTER 4
PRICE YOUR BOOK

Summary

Let's put all those numbers in a chart. Note that every scenario gives you a higher royalty rate than a traditional publisher's royalty of 4% to 10%.

Sales Channel	Selling Price	Royalty $	Royalty %	# of Books to Break Even
Ebook				
Regular price	$4.99	$3.49	70%	592
Regular price at KDP	$4.99	$3.35	70%	617
Sale/promotion price at KDP	$0.99	$0.35	35%	5,900
Sale/promotion price at other retailers	$0.99	$0.70	70%	2,950
Print Book				
Direct to reader at a book signing with sale price	$10.00	$3.47	35%	595
Direct to reader via KDP	$17.99	$6.35	35%	326
A bookstore or library buys a book via KDP	$17.99	$2.75	15%	751
A bookstore or library buys a book via IngramSpark	$17.99	$7.67	45%	269

Figure 12: Comparing print book royalties

Links

KDP has a beta app available, Pricing Support (Beta).
   https://kdp.amazon.com/en_US/help/topic/G201551180
Alliance of Independent Authors
   https://selfpublishingadvice.org/how-indie-authors-set-paperback-prices/

Your Assignment

Let's go back to that book you priced edits for in Chapter 1. Use the page count in your manuscript but know that the number will change significantly when the book is formatted.

Go to www.IngramSpark.com, find the tools, and calculate the three print scenarios. Use the same print options as shown in Figure 13 in Appendix B: Sample Pricing; we'll talk more about their meaning later.

Go to KDP Help https://kdp.amazon.com/en_US/help/topic/G201834330, find the tools, and calculate the three print scenarios.

Record your answers in the Pricing Chart in Appendix A: Data Sheets.

Chapter 5
Print Your Book

WHY DO A PRINT BOOK?

Because everybody says you have to.

True, but that doesn't answer the question.

Picture this...

Two hundred authors are sitting at tables in a big conference room. Hundreds of readers are strolling the room, laughing and chatting to their favourite authors. They're also on the hunt for new favourites.

You're an ebook only author. You have clever colourful postcards fanned out on the table with links and a QR code leading directly to your website or your retailers. There's even a coupon code. Your smile is friendly, your pen is in hand, ready to sign.

Except... people are going right by you and stopping three authors down where there are stacks of print books.

Why are they doing that? Your story is as good as, possibly better than, that other writer.

People strolling a book-signing are drawn to real books; they can pick them up, touch them, get them signed, pay you, and buy a real thing. There's a social interaction happening. Those browsing folk aren't drawn to post cards; there's no heft to them. All too often, valuable post cards are tossed away with all the other swag. A real book is kept and read and maybe passed around to family and friends or handed in to the local library for even more people to read.

I've seen it over and over again.

And the thrill... oh, my... the absolute *thrill* of holding your first print book in your hands... very few things can beat that! Your hours of effort and angst to craft the perfect story, the agony of decision over cover design, the conquering of KDP, D2D, and IngramSpark, have all coalesced into *your* book in *your* hands.

The Jargon

The first time you load your print book files to a printer's website can be daunting, all that publishing jargon. Here's a guide to what the terms mean and the standard choices for self-published works.

Trade or Mass Market

The usual paperback novel is released in American mass-market format, approximately 4" x 6" with newsprint-like pages. The majority of self-published works are released in trade paperback, in a larger size, with higher quality paper.

Trim Size

When manufacturing a book, the edges of the pages don't always line up perfectly, so the book comes off the printing press a bit bigger and is then trimmed, nice and neat, to the finished size of your trade paperback book. There are a number of standard sizes, 6" x 9" being the most common.

Interior Colour and Paper

There are two elements here, the colour of the content (text, pictures) and the colour of the paper. After selecting the colour of the content, a few more items will pop open. These are for the colour of the paper.

Colour

The standard is black and white. Children's illustrated books and coffee table books will be full colour. For other books, your formatter should have given you a black and white PDF with all images in grayscale. IngramSpark often throws an error about colour profile. If your file is black and white, you can safely accept the error and move on.

Paper

White paper is standard. It's thinner paper, so it's less expensive to print and ship. Cream paper is thicker, more expensive to print and ship, and can sometimes be a little too yellow. Your cover designer calculated the spine width based on the chosen paper. In January 2020, IngramSpark announced the addition of groundwood paper in limited sizes from select US facilities. I'm assuming that's like the standard newsprint-like paper you see in mass market books.

If you're using colour images, cream paper will distort the colour.

There are regional preferences for paper colour; in the UK, cream paper is preferred. So check with a local writers' group.

Bleed

When an image goes to the very edge of the page like in a picture book, the image is said to bleed. If your book has page margins, you do not have bleed.

Binding Type

This refers to how the pages are attached to each other. Perfect bound (the standard) is glued together. Saddle stitching puts staples down the centre of a slender book of less than 48 pages; this is sometimes called a chapbook.

IngramSpark also offers hard cover with a case laminate cover (the cover image is glued to the boards) and/or a dust jacket.

Laminate Type

Choose either glossy or matte finish for your paperback cover. Current trends favour a matte finish.

This is not the same as the case laminated binding. You can have a case laminate binding with a glossy or matte laminate finish.

Page Count

The number of pages as shown in the PDF viewer, including both sides of the paper. Must be an even number.

Pricing

For information on pricing your print book, see Chapter 4: Price Your Book.

Proof Copy

With so many print-on-demand (POD) books coming off the presses, it's inevitable that mistakes will happen. I've seen fancy fonts print as squares, incorrect trim sizes, weird colours that had little to do with the original covers, misaligned cover spines....

Always, ALWAYS, order a proof copy. Then if something should go wonky, you can take a photo and send it as proof of poor printing. And then the printer can't wag a finger and say, "You should have ordered a proof".

CHAPTER 5
PRINT YOUR BOOK

HOW MANY COPIES TO ORDER

After the proof is set, don't get carried away and order boxes of books. Money that would be better spent on marketing is tied up in those boxes. You'll have to store them somewhere safe, no floods or bugs or dogs.

Unless you have a gigantic circle of family and friends salivating to get their hands on your book, don't order more than ten or twenty at a time. Then if you change your cover, you won't have a lot of out-dated stock to deal with.

YOUR ASSIGNMENT

Review your choices at your chosen printer/distributor and complete the Print Book Details in Appendix A: Data Sheets.

Chapter 6
Publish Your Book

By publish, I mean set up your retailer account, load your book files, enter your metadata, set your price and territories, and click the publish button.

GOING WIDE

The expression "going wide" refers to the distribution of your book.

When you load your book to KDP, you have a choice to enter the KDP Select program (https://kdp.amazon.com/en_US/help/topic/G200798990). There are several benefits when you sign up, like higher royalty rates and exclusive marketing opportunities. But there's a trade-off; you're not allowed to load your book anywhere else; you're exclusive to KDP Select. Declining this exclusivity means you can go wide. If you try to trick KDP and do both exclusive and wide, you run the risk of having your KDP account cancelled. So make your choice in advance. Some authors swear by KDP Select, others want exposure to as many markets as possible. Ask for opinions to make an informed choice.

There are many aggregators that will distribute your book to a wide marketplace, Kobo, Draft2Digital, IngramSpark. Sometimes the lists will overlap and not all vendors have ways to deal with the conflict.

The ISBN is the most common way that vendors avoid duplicates.

If the ISBN coming from IngramSpark matches a file already present, the transfer *might* not proceed. KDP checks for this, so load all versions of your book in KDP *before* your load to IngramSpark. Kobo does not, so either don't load direct to Kobo or don't publish your ebook on IngramSpark. It's not a happy decision to make.

Mix and Match

Some authors will choose to print paperback and hardback versions of their books. Some will also have different sizes for these versions.

It's grand to offer your readers a wide choice, but each version will require its own interior PDF and exterior cover and that's an expense to you. Refer back to Chapter 2: Prepare Your Book for details.

Deciding on one size for both paperback and hardback allows you to use the same interior file for both versions. Though separate covers will still be required. A separate file is also required for a dust jacket.

Libraries love large print books, so think about adding the format to your list. Separate interior and cover files are required.

Separate ISBNs will also be required for each version.

Retailer Account

Setting up the retailer account is pretty straight forward, it's your personal information, your tax identification number (SSN, SIN etc.), and banking information.

> Accounts created, files loaded, prices set... now you're a publisher!

Each of the retailers will have their own rules about when your royalties are paid out. Some will accept PayPal, others want a bank.

The trickiest part is correctly identifying your bank's electronic code. That's the code you'll see across the bottom of cheques or on the paperwork for your account.

There can be difficulty around payments in currencies other than US$ in the royalties paid via wire transfer. The cost of the wire transfer can wipe out the royalty amount. One suggestion around this is to open an account with an online US bank. You can leave the money in that account or do an inter-bank transfer to move the funds to your regular account. Do your research carefully to ensure everything will work they way you want it to.

ITIN & W8-BEN

The tax interview is a lot of fun as well (not), especially for non-US citizens.

First, a bit of detail about non-residents selling via American retailers. Over the years, the United States has signed a number of reciprocal tax treaties with a bunch of countries that breaks down to an agreement not to withhold earnings for income tax in each others' countries, provided the exemption can be proved.

That's where ITINs and W8-BENs come in.

The Individual Tax Identification Number (ITIN) is a Social Security Number (SSN) for non-residents of the US. The ITIN does what it says on the box, identifies you as a real person, living in another country, who is receiving payments from an American company. The Internal Revenue Service (IRS) does the investigation and issues the ITIN when they are satisfied you meet their criteria.

After you get an ITIN, a W8-BEN form is completed every two years or so for the retailer (Amazon et al) issuing the payment. It states the type of payment (royalties) and the country (Canada et al) with whom the tax treaty has been signed. This is the retailer's assurance that you are still exempt from withholding.

In 2015, KDP started accepting Canadian Social Insurance Numbers (SIN) as proof of identity. Check the help documents for each retailer's requirements to ensure you get it right.

Your obligation to uphold the international treaty is to report American income to your country's revenue agency on your tax reporting form (for Canada, that's the CRA and T4 respectively) in the currency of your country. Look for currency conversion rates and rules on your tax agency's website. The American retailer will send you a statement of earnings or you can download the report via the company's dashboard.

For instructions on getting an ITIN and completing a W8-BEN, refer to my article "How to Get an ITIN" at https://wovenred.wordpress.com/articles-for-writers/how-to-get-an-itin/.

The process is the same for anyone in any country where tax treaties have been signed. There are links in the article to the IRS where you can get complete details.

I'm sure somebody somewhere could give me a list of pros and cons, but the way I look at it is, I'll do whatever makes it easier for retailers to pay me. Getting an ITIN doesn't cost anything but time.

If taxes have been withheld, the only way to get them back is to complete a US tax return, a nightmare for non-residents from all I've heard.

Finally, I am not a lawyer of any stripe, so do seek expert opinion and assistance if needed.

Book Files

We've already talked about covers and manuscript files in Chapter 2: Prepare Your Book. You'll have two files for your ebook (jpeg cover and epub content) and two PDF files for your print book (cover and content).

Metadata

Metadata is data about data. For a book, the story is the data, so metadata is information about your story. Most of metadata is self-explanatory when you get to the appropriate page in the upload sequence. Save time and frustration; gather your metadata on the form provided in Appendix A: Data Sheets before you begin.

The full list of metadata is:
- title
- subtitle
- series name, if appropriate
- book's number in the series, if appropriate
- edition, starts at one

- author name or pseudonym
- contributors if more than one author
- back cover blurb
- keywords
- categories
- age and grade range, if appropriate
- ISBN
- publisher (you!)
- price
- territories

Some of these are optional. I've seen a slightly controversial use of the subtitle to clarify and expand the genre right up front, e.g., a small-town reunion novel. Keywords and categories (BISAC codes) require more explanation.

Keywords

Keywords are words or phrases that readers use to search for books on a website. You used keywords when hunting for an image back in Chapter 2. They're in addition to the basic data of title, author, and genre. Phrases, or strings, are more searchable than single words, e.g., contemporary romance vs romance. Good keywords can improve discoverability, so readers can find your books.

Keywords are so important, that a whole science has developed around them; articles abound, and books have been written. At the end of the chapter are some links that will get you started.

BISAC Codes

The Book Industry Study Group, Inc. was incorporated in February 1975 to improve research capabilities within the publishing industry. The BISAC Subject Headings List, also known as the BISAC Subject Codes List (https://bisg.org/page/bisacedition), categorizes books based on content. It standardizes database searches and guides the shelf placement of a book in a bricks and mortar store.

The list is updated annually and is so useful that many retailers use it as is, though Amazon adds their own categories from time to time.

Make it part of your annual book status review to check if any changes have been made to your benefit.

Price

We talked a lot about pricing and royalties in Chapter 4: Price Your Book.

On KDP's pricing page, you'll find a really cool tool. The KDP Pricing Support shows a graph of the relationship between price, past sales, and author earnings for KDP books similar yours. Click the View Service button. If you like the results, click the Yes button under the graph.

Territories

This is about selling your book in all the countries and currencies where your retailer does business. Amazon is American but has websites based in other countries, U.K., Brazil, Germany etc. Kobo is owned by Rakuten who recently made a deal with WalMart and has agreements with other companies around the world.

There are sales tax implications when selling globally. The retailer will calculate applicable sales tax based on the reader's location. In the European Union, consumers expect to see the Value Added Tax (VAT) included in the book price. Most retailers will take care of calculating, displaying, collecting, and remitting the tax for you.

Most retailers will also convert your list price based on currency rates at the time you load your book. I can't find any information on how fluctuations in world currencies are managed.

Links

Articles:
JaneFriedman.com: Optimizing Amazon Keywords
https://www.janefriedman.com/optimizing-books-amazon-keyword-search/

Books:
How to Sell Books by the Truckload on Amazon by Penny Sansevieri
https://www.amazon.com/How-Sell-Books-Truckload-Amazon-ebook/dp/B075WL33XB/

Amazon Decoded by David Gaughran FREE!
http://davidgaughran.com/books/amazon-decoded/

Your Assignment

Do your keyword and BISAC code research and record your findings in the Metadata chart in Appendix A: Data Sheets.

Chapter 7
Putting It All Together

STEP BY STEP

As the publisher, you have ultimate control over, and responsibility for, the quality of the book you're about to release. Quality takes time.

> Save yourself the anxiety. Finish the book, get it edited, formatted, covered, priced, and loaded...
> THEN announce your pre-order and release dates.

Even though you've completed your book, there's still a long way to go and, honestly, your schedule is your team's schedule. Each step is reliant on the one before it. Each step can be derailed, making a mess of everything that comes after.

Do you have a release date in mind? Number one piece of advice I've learned the hard way: Do NOT announce that date just yet. Think of it as a guideline, no more.

Way back at the beginning of the book, I talked about the interdependency of the steps. Let's put them in sequential order.

1) Finish the manuscript. Make it the best you can with the help of beta readers and critique groups.
2) Send the manuscript to your developmental editor at least three days before the date your book comes up on her schedule. Confirm the delivery date of your edits.
3) On receipt of the edited file, update your manuscript.
4) If you've arranged it, send it back to the editor for the second round of developmental edits. Confirm the delivery date.
5) Pay your editor.
6) Update your manuscript.
7) Complete Autocrit edits.
8) Complete hardcopy edits.

9) Complete read back edits.
10) If you've arranged it, send out your manuscript for copyedits and proofread. This is often the same person who will do both at the same time.
11) Pay your editor.
12) Get your ISBNs.
13) Determine your print book trim size, paper colour, and cover laminate.
14) Write and edit your front and back matter, including the blurb. For a complete list of what your formatter needs, see https://wovenred.wordpress.com/2016/06/13/formatter-requirements/.
15) Send information sheets to the cover designer at least three days before the date your book comes up on her schedule. Confirm the delivery date.
16) Review your covers, request changes.
17) Pay your cover designer.
18) Send ebook cover and manuscript with back and front matter to the formatter at least three days before the date your book comes up on her schedule. Confirm the delivery date.
19) Review and approve your formatted files.
20) Pay your formatter.
21) Calculate your prices.
22) Send final page count, page colour, cover laminate, price, ISBN, and blurb for the print book to your cover designer. Confirm the delivery date.
23) Do one final review of all your files. This is your last chance. Take your time.
24) Send your book files out to the reviewers you've lined up. Confirm the dates when the reviews will be posted.
25) Load your book files to retailers in either pre-order or published status. The ebook files can be loaded in a couple of days. The print book files have to go through an approvals process that may require your getting back to the formatter and cover designer, so give yourself a week just in case something goes wrong. Don't publish the print book until after you've ordered, examined, and approved the proof copy. This review may also require you to get back to the formatter and cover designer.
26) NOW announce your release date.

CHAPTER 7
PUTTING IT ALL TOGETHER

TIPS

Note the target and completion dates in the schedule provided in Appendix C: The Schedule. Then you'll have a reference for next time.

1) Don't announce your release date until everything done. Yes, I've said this before. Pay heed. I've seen far too many desperate authors scrambling for freelancers and making do because of unforeseen events.
2) Promptly review each set of files as you receive them.
3) Keep you team informed. The sooner, the better. If something goes sideways, inform your freelancers so they can adjust their own schedules accordingly.
4) The one overlap in the schedule will be the cover designer, who can get started while you're in DIY edits.
5) Be patient.
6) Pay your freelancers promptly.

Appendices

The following appendices are provided to assist with the assignments at the end of each chapter and to help you manage your book release from the moment you type "The End" to the moment you click Publish.

APPENDIX A: DATA SHEETS

Services Used

Service	Estimated Cost	Actual Cost	Service Provider, URLs, notes
Editing, round #1			
Editing, round #2			
Editing, round #3			
Printing for edits			
Cover			
Formatting			
ISBNs			
Copyright Registration			
TOTAL			

APPENDIX A: DATA SHEETS

Metadata

Title	
Subtitle	
Series name	
Book's number in the series	
Edition	
Author name or pseudonym	
Contributors if more than one author	
Back cover blurb file name	
Keywords	
Categories	
Age and grade range	
ISBN provider	
ISBN Epub	
ISBN Mobi	
ISBN Print	
ISBN Audio	
Publisher (you!)	
Publisher contact information	

Copyright

Year of copyright	
Owner of copyright	
Copyright issuer	
Date copyright submitted and received	
Disclaimer	
Photo credit and link	
Artist credit and link	
Cover credit and link	
Editor credit and link	
Formatter credit and link	

Print Book Details

Complete a chart for each print version you're publishing.

Trim size	
Interior colour	
Interior paper	
Bleed	
Binding type	
Laminate type	
Page count	

Appendix A: Data Sheets

Pricing

Add another section for hardback and audio if you're also releasing those.

Sales Channel	Selling Price	Royalty $	Royalty %	# of Books to Break Even
Ebook				
Regular price				
Regular price at KDP				
Sale/promotion price at KDP				
Sale/promotion price at other retailers				
Print Book				
Direct to reader at a book signing with sale price				
Direct to reader via KDP				
A bookstore or library buys a book via KDP				
A bookstore or library buys a book via IngramSpark				

Appendix B: Sample Pricing

Trim Size	6.000" x 9.000" (229mm x 152mm)

Interior Color and Paper	● Black & White
	   ● White B&W: printed on 50lb White paper
	   ○ Creme B&W: printed on 50lb Creme paper
	   ○ Groundwood B&W: printed on 38lb Eggshell paper (mass market-like)
	○ Color

Binding Type	● Paperback
	   ● Perfect Bound Glued spine with color laminated cover
	   ○ Saddle Stitch Stapled pages with color laminated cover, 4-48 page count
	○ Hardback

Laminate Type	● Gloss Cover or dust jacket ○ Matte Cover or dust jacket ○ Textured Digital cloth only, no dust jacket
Page Count	300 (Multiple of 2, between 18 and 1200)
List Price	17.99 $
Wholesale Discount	30 %
Market	Global Connect
Print Charge	$ 4.92 ←
Publisher Compensation	$ 7.67 ←

Important Note: All Print Charges and Publisher compensation amounts shown are exclusive of GST or any other taxes.

Figure 13: Publisher compensation calculation

Appendix B: Sample Pricing

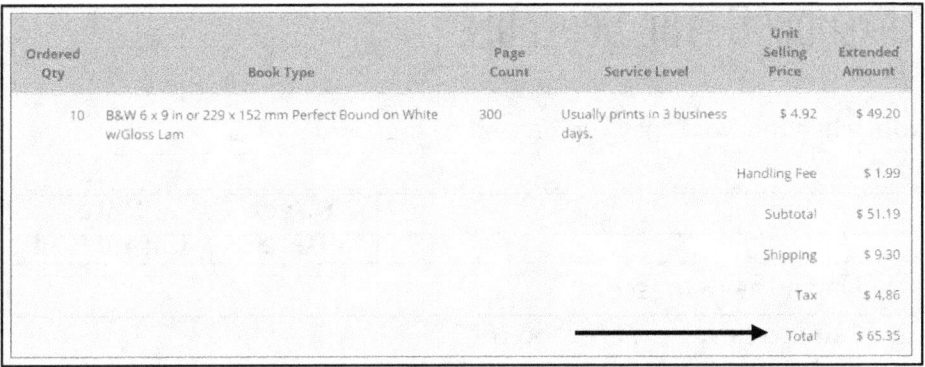

Figure 15: Print & ship calculation

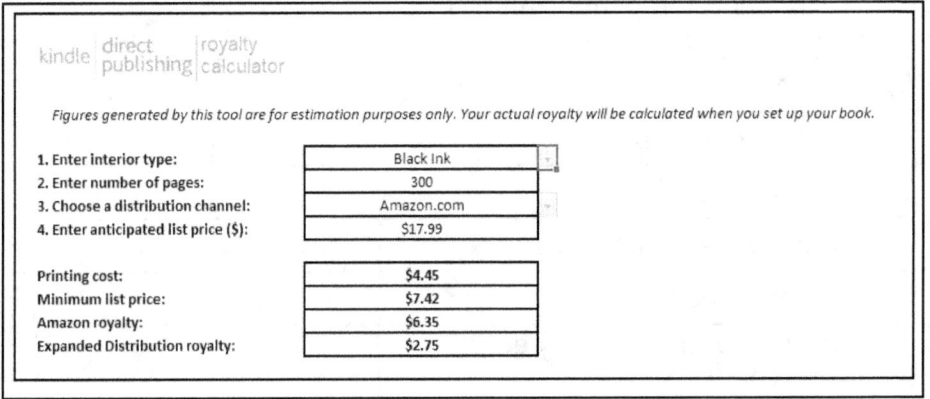

Figure 14: KDP print book pricing

Note: KDP doesn't include trim size in the estimates. Based on old calculations in CreateSpace, I'm guessing it's using 6" x 9".

Appendix C: The Schedule

Note when the word "pay" occurs and be prepared.

Task	Target Date	Date Completed
1) Finish the manuscript		
2) Send to developmental editor for first round		
3) Update your manuscript		
4) Send to developmental editor for second round		
5) **Pay** your developmental editor		
6) Update your manuscript		
7) Complete Autocrit edits		
8) Complete hardcopy edits		
9) Complete read back edits		
10) Send manuscript to copy editor/ proofreader		
11) **Pay** your copy editor/ proofreader		
12) Get your ISBNs		
13) Determine trim size, paper, cover laminate		
14) Write front and back matter		
15) Send information sheets to the cover designer		
16) Review and approve cover designs		
17) **Pay** your cover designer		
18) Send files to the formatter		

Appendix C: The Schedule

Task	Target Date	Date Completed
19) Review and approve formatted files		
20) **Pay** your formatter		
21) Calculate your prices		
22) Send print book details to cover designer		
23) One last careful review		
24) Send your book files out to the reviewers		
25) Load files to vendors		
26) Announce your release date		

Appendix D: Resources

My personal go-to list of authorities on self-publishing.

Alliance of Independent Authors
https://www.allianceindependentauthors.org/

David Gaughran's Blog
http://davidgaughran.com/blog/

IngramSpark Self-Publishing
http://www.ingramspark.com/

Kindle Direct Publishing
https://kdp.amazon.com/en_US/?ref_=NFD_TN_si

Kristine Kathryn Rusch: Business Rusch Publishing Articles
https://kriswrites.com/business-rusch-publishing-articles/

Kobo Writing Life
https://kobowritinglife.com/

The Creative Penn
https://www.thecreativepenn.com/

The Book Designer
https://www.thebookdesigner.com/

The Passive Voice
http://www.thepassivevoice.com/

Writer Beware
https://accrispin.blogspot.com/

About Joan Frantschuk

Joan has worked with most versions of MS Word, creating user documents with all the bells and whistles. When she began writing fiction, MS Word was the easy part.

After releasing her second title, writing under the pseudonym Joan Leacott, Joan put her newly honed formatting skills to use for her friends and Woven Red was born.

Ms. Frantschuk is a member of the Romance Writers of America and the Toronto Romance Writers.

Joan writes, and proudly self-publishes, contemporary multi-generational novels featuring the lives, loves, and scandals of small-town Clarence Bay, Canada. Check out Joan's books on her website www.JoanLeacott.ca.

Mastering Word for Fiction Writers

WovenRed.Teachable.com

I just finished up "Mastering Word for Fiction Writers" with Joan. Bar none, this is the best writing course I have ever taken. The ability to fully use the features of the program enriches my writing by making it less stressful. Wish I'd done this years ago. Thanks, Joan, for your expert guidance on this program. ~ Ane Ryan Walker

I've been using Word for over twenty years, but I now realize there was so much I didn't know! Joan's plain-language lessons were comprehensive, well-illustrated and made sense. Her readiness to provide detailed answers to thorny/specific questions was incredibly helpful. She provided insights into this powerful but often infuriatingly quirky application with confidence and good humour. Kudos, Joan. I'm recommending your workshop to everyone I know who uses Word regularly. ~ Hyacinthe Miller

This definitive online course is the perfect complement to creative writing. It will save you time, energy, and money by teaching you how to use Microsoft Word with power.

The two self-study course packages, available individually or in money-saving bundles, follow the life cycle of a book from rough draft, through editing and critiquing, and on to submission to contests or agents and editors. If self-publishing is your chosen path, there are courses for converting your manuscript to an ebook or print book.

1. The lessons include:
2. best practices for Word setup and usage,
3. in-depth explanation of the Word techniques,

Appendix D: Resources

4. working documents for doing the step-by-step exercises,
5. review documents to check your work,
6. six custom Word templates.

In the core competencies package (12 lessons in two courses) for ALL writers, you will master:
1. Styles for consistent text and chapter headings,
2. Navigation Pane to click from chapter to chapter, scene to scene,
3. automatic Table of Contents to create a synopsis in THREE steps,
4. AutoFormat and AutoCorrect to speed up your writing,
5. Spelling and Grammar settings customized for fiction writers,
6. Track Changes to enjoy hassle-free critiques and beta reads.

Or go hard-core and register for the Complete Mastering Word for Fiction Writers package that includes all 32 lessons in all five courses.
1. Section Breaks to create a clean contest entry or agent/editor submission,
2. Compatible layout to convert your manuscript to an epub or mobi file,
3. Page Layout and custom Styles to design a beautiful print book to sign with pride.
4. Plus, you can get a personal review of your formatted files to make sure you did it right!
5. Plus, continuing online support with the instructor or a private Facebook group.

WHAT'S TEACHABLE?
Teachable is to online courses what Wordpress is to websites, a well-respected, well-funded, and well-supported platform for course creators to present incredible workshops. Find out more at www.Teachable.com

www.ingramcontent.com/pod-product-compliance
Lightning Source LLC
Chambersburg PA
CBHW071502070526
44578CB00001B/412